About Demos

Demos is a greenhouse for new ideas which can improve the quality of our lives. As an independent think tank, we aim to create an open resource of knowledge and learning that operates beyond traditional party politics.

We connect researchers, thinkers and practitioners to an international network of people changing politics. Our ideas regularly influence government policy, but we also work with companies, NGOs, colleges and professional bodies.

Demos knowledge is organised around five themes, which combine to create new perspectives. The themes are democracy, learning, enterprise, quality of life and global change.

But we also understand that thinking by itself is not enough. Demos has helped to initiate a number of practical projects which are delivering real social benefit through the redesign of public services.

We bring together people from a wide range of backgrounds to cross-fertilise ideas and experience. By working with Demos, our partners develop a sharper insight into the way ideas shape society. For Demos, the process is as important as the final product.

www.demos.co.uk

First published in 2005 by Demos and the Scottish Book Trust
© Demos
Some rights reserved – see copyright licence for details

ISBN 1 84180 138 0
Copy edited by Julie Pickard
Typeset by Land & Unwin, Bugbrooke
Printed by HenDI Systems, London

For further information and
subscription details please contact:

Demos
Magdalen House
136 Tooley Street
London SE1 2TU

telephone: 0845 458 5949
email: hello@demos.co.uk
web: www.demos.co.uk

Scotland 2020

Hopeful stories for a northern nation

Edited by
Gerry Hassan
Eddie Gibb
Lydia Howland

With a foreword by George Reid MSP

DEMOS

DEM⊚S

Contents

To retreat behind the notion that the audience simply wants to dump its troubles at the door and escape reality is a cowardly abandonment of the artist's responsibility. Story isn't a flight from reality but a vehicle that carries us on our search for reality, our best effort to make sense out of the reality of existence.

Robert McKee
Story: Substance, structure, style and the principles of screenwriting

Acknowledgements

In the last year, the Scotland 2020 programme has weaved its way around the country – a bit like a modern travelling road show – engaging in discussions and conversation about the future, how to think creatively about it, and the future of Scotland. It has been our pleasure over that period to discuss some of these issues, ideas and thoughts with the people mentioned here, and many more besides.

First of all we would like to acknowledge the project partners who made Scotland 2020 possible, and should probably point out that the conclusions of the project are ours and do not necessarily represent the policies of any of the partner organisations. So thanks are due to: Michael Bird, British Council Scotland; Sandy Brady, Highlands and Islands Enterprise; Brendan Dick, BT Scotland; John Downie, Federation of Small Businesses; Ashley Evans, Electronics Scotland; Ewan Mearns, Scottish Enterprise; Martin Raymond, NHS Health Scotland; Jane Richardson, Oracle Corporation UK; Gavin Wallace, Scottish Arts Council; and Steve Youd-Thomas, The Co-operative Group.

We would particularly like to thank Marc Lambert and his team at the Scottish Book Trust who hosted several events during the course of the project, and put us in touch with the fiction writers who contributed to this book.

A project like Scotland 2020 is an exercise in which many people gave their time, ideas and enthusiasm. In particular, the following people all gave valuable insights and support at key moments during the project: Alex Bell, Shona Cormack, Carol Craig, Jane Denholm, Jerome de Groot, Phil Hanlon, Christopher Harvie, Elinor Kelly, Faith Liddell, Jim McCormick, Susan McPhee, Tom Nairn, Robert Rae, Nigel Smith, Jean Urquhart and Andy Wightman.

We would like to thank Keir Bloomer and his team at Clackmannanshire Council for partnering us on the Scotland 2020: An Adaptive State event in Alloa, and also the very hospitable staff of Gean House in Alloa.

At Demos numerous people contributed ideas and encouragement to the project. Matthew Horne facilitated two scenario-building workshops with his usual skill, and helped us to understand 'futures literacy'. After reading an early draft of the introduction, Paul Skidmore literally gave us 'hope', which became an important concept in our thinking. Thanks also to Paul Miller and Melissa Mean who gave valuable insights.

Throughout, Claire Ghoussoub did a fantastic job of developing and maintaining a 'community of interest' around the project, and made several events happen against the odds. And Tom Bentley, the director of Demos, encouraged us throughout the project and then helped us to say what we really meant.

The people who copyedited, proofread and typeset this book deserve particular thanks: Julie Pickard, Susannah Wight and John Unwin of Land & Unwin.

Finally we would like to thank all the people of Nairn who took part in Nairn Day and made it such a success. It was the defining event of the project, and helped to convince us that futures thinking is an activity that everyone in Scotland can and should get involved in.

Gerry Hassan
Eddie Gibb
Lydia Howland
February 2005
gerry.hassan@virgin.net
eddie.gibb@demos.co.uk

Foreword

George Reid MSP

Holyrood is certainly not Westminster. In its architecture, practice and procedures the new Scottish Parliament has been deliberately designed for new models of 21st century participative governance.

It is not a patrician building, standing proudly apart, where elected representatives face each other two swords' lengths across the floor of a Commons Chamber which still echoes with the set-piece debates of the 19th century and earlier.

Instead, Holyrood is an integral part of Edinburgh's Royal Mile – a place of nooks and crannies where people and politicians can come together.

Its Chamber feels distinctly European. Members – spread across six parties and a group of five independents – sit in the round. The public galleries, pleasingly full much of the time, sweep down virtually to the floor.

It is a parliamentary campus, said its architect Enric Miralles, designed for shared conversations not for sterile confrontations.

Indeed, in its extensive engagement with the people of Scotland in its pre-legislative hearings and acclaimed system of public petitioning (even electronically, online), the Scottish Parliament has been the subject of worldwide interest in how it is putting participation into practice.

The engagement with civic and voluntary Scotland has been

intense and sustained. It has been less so, to date, with Scotland's entrepreneurs, academics, artists and free-thinkers.

Yet these are the people who will help shape our common future. The people best placed to answer the question: how do we build a sustainable society, comfortable with itself at home, and confident of competing in the global marketplace?

It is said that the future belongs to those who prepare for it. This is not easy in an age of great complexity and genuine uncertainty – when decision-making processes are layered and shared throughout an interconnected world of rapid economic, environmental, demographic and cultural change. And when classic models of government are giving way to looser forms of governance.

At the official opening of our new parliament, I described Holyrood as the place that will shape Scotland's future. I warned of the Caledonian Cringe, the reluctance to take risks to secure that future. And I trusted that, in our new legislature, we would have the courage to face the enemy – and have the wisdom to know that often it is us.

The Demos project gently explores this issue and looks at the Scots uneasiness in expressing themselves in positive ways. It is a fascinating model of what can be achieved at community level in generating optimism and learning about our country's future prospects. The book is a timely and valuable addition to Scotland's futures debate.

The Parliament is now developing its own Futures Forum. Its job is not to promote any specific or official view of what that future is – but simply to encourage our citizens, and foreign guests, to think out of the box and over the horizon about where our country is heading.

In so doing, they will help us to perceive where we are now, and where we should be going.

The Rt Hon George Reid MSP is the Presiding Officer of the Scottish Parliament

1. Scotland 2020: The Power of Hope

Gerry Hassan and Eddie Gibb

A unique feature of human consciousness is its inclusion of the future. Expectations strongly affect all aspects of human functioning. . . . Hope inspires a feeling of well-being and is a spur to action. Hopelessness, the inability to imagine a tolerable future, is a powerful motive for suicide.

Jerome Frank, 'The role of hope in psychotherapy'[1]

Introduction

Scotland is a nation of narrators who tell and retell each other stories that turn into modern myths. Some myths have a power that changes behaviour: the Tartan Army have told themselves that they are the best football fans in the world so often that they have created a collective culture that promotes good behaviour among travelling supporters. In this essay, we consider how the stories Scotland tells about itself today have a bearing on tomorrow.

People of all countries tell themselves stories, of course. Stories allow ideas, myths and folktales to gain power through their constant telling and retelling, and passing down through generations. This can be seen in national discourse – the American dream, Poland's sense of itself as a 'chosen country' and the Irish 'Celtic Tiger'.

Scotland has a number of these stories – the belief in an egalitarian ethos, the 'democratic intellect' shaped by the potential liberating hand of education, and a collectivist sense of looking after the most vulnerable. In recent years, particularly since the establishment of the Scottish Parliament in 1999, Scotland's dominant stories and the way they are told have become increasingly problematic: as we argue later, pessimism has turned into fatalism.

We suggest that a useful antidote to this fatalism is the ability to think imaginatively about the future – or 'futures literacy', as we have called it. Imagining a better future for an individual or for a nation is a first step in creating one. Here we discuss how that capacity to imagine the future can be developed in Scotland.

Many Scottish institutions have already conducted exercises in futures thinking and Scotland 2020 is a project that has used futures thinking to explore the narratives through which Scottish aspirations are projected. It emphasised stories and storytelling, commissioning fiction writers alongside more traditional forms of scenario-building.

We believe that constructing new stories about Scotland is not just about the quality of the vision, but the way the story is created. Our main conclusion is that Scots from all walks of life and corners of the land need to be involved in a 'mass imagination' exercise that develops new, shared stories about Scotland's future.

Looking back to the future

Fifteen years ago – the same time frame that we are looking forward – the main animating idea of Scottish politics was the redeeming power of the Scottish Parliament. But the shared aspiration for a Parliament has not been matched by an enthusiasm for the actions of the institution itself or the actors who inhabit it.

This negative response has specific Scottish conditions, but also taps into a wider global pessimism, which goes well beyond the merits or not of devolution. A new political culture and ethos has not flowed from new institutions and processes. Devolution has not restored faith in politics in the way that had been hoped, and any sense of shared optimism about a different kind of political culture in Scotland is waning. Instead, the experience of recent years has strengthened the powers of pessimism and fatalism.

Why should this be? We suggest that there are three Scotlands, which can help us to understand the stories we are told. *Traditional Scotland* is characterised by pessimism about the future, due to the erosion of distinctively Scottish values. It may not be the official story, but it pervades much of Scottish public life. *Modernist Scotland* is the official vision of the future based on an optimistic view of the benefits of economic growth. Scotland's 'official future' has the backing of government institutions but most Scots do not enthusiastically subscribe to it.

The third emerging Scotland is the subject of this essay: we have called it *hopeful Scotland* because it is optimistic about the future while acknowledging its unpredictability. In a hopeful Scotland, unqualified optimism would be replaced by 'learned optimism'. In the process, its sense of what is possible, both individually and collectively, would be transformed.

That is why a new understanding of futures literacy, and how to cultivate it, is crucial to a renewed sense of possibility and shared hope. In the rest of this essay we explore the three Scotlands, analyse the experience of engaging local communities in futures thinking, and make recommendations for future investments in futures thinking.

The three Scotlands

There are two Scotlands, the traditionalist and modernist, with which people are familiar, but a third – hopeful – has begun to emerge. The characteristics of the three Scotlands are:

O **Traditionalist** – This is conservative with a small 'c', can be left, right, centre or not think of itself in these terms and is opposed to the claims of modernisation. Whether this is Old Labour fighting to retain a more collectivist approach, traditional Nationalists seeing Scottish identity being eroded or the Catholic Church opposing social reforms, there is a common strand of resisting the encroachment of the modern world. Some of them hanker after a supposed past defined by certainty.

○ **Modernist** – This is the 'official future' of Scotland. This is the world of government, public agencies, 'the system' and the idea of change as 'the machine'. The focus is on institutional notions of change, policy delivery and levers. Seeming truths such as 'the knowledge economy' and 'growth as a policy priority' are discussed in agenda-setting, aspirational documents such as 'Smart, Successful Scotland'. While modernist Scotland invokes the mantra of 'change' constantly, it reinforces a deeply conventional and orthodox view of the world.

○ **Hopeful** – This is an emerging and increasingly influential group, the least homogeneous of the three and containing people within 'the system' as well as artists, thinkers and imagineers. It argues that 'the machine' way has been tried and found wanting, and that we need to embrace a different approach based on hope, deep change and complexity.

The three Scotlands think in fundamentally different ways about the future. Paradoxically both the traditionalist and modernist accounts of Scotland share a marked sense of fatalism, springing from the belief that the future is an inevitable continuation of present trends. Geoff Mulgan has described the damage which fatalism can bring about:

Fatalism is the worst thing that can happen to any area. And fatalism is the worst thing that can happen to any society. That's why retaining the confidence that the world is malleable, that what looks natural is wholly man made, is the greatest gift that the policy community can offer.[2]

The traditionalist perspective believes that what makes Scotland distinctive is being slowly eroded. In it, Scotland ceases to exist as a place different from anywhere else in the world, and culture, traditions and identity are seen as fragile and under constant attack.

In this world, Scottish distinctiveness is always under threat from something or someone, whether it is social reformers wanting to liberalise attitudes and services to sexual health, or New Labour economic reforms being seen as weakening collectivist values.

The modernist perspective is based on the idea that Scotland's future is positive if it can follow a diagnosis based on embracing economic growth and an individualised, marketised, consumption-based view of the world. The Australian academic Richard Eckersley calls this a 'go for growth linear optimism' which unquestioningly assumes that tomorrow will always be better than today if we continue to embrace and accelerate economic growth.[3]

It is also a technocratic, soulless and managerial vision of the world which is silent on important aspects of human well-being, emotional, social and spiritual. This is a world of winners and losers, where failure is seen as personal, permanent and pervasive, and people are left feeling they are powerless, as helplessness turns into hopelessness. The modernist world is one that does not encourage hope.

The third perspective – hopeful Scotland – is characterised by a sense of optimism, but of a very different kind from the modernists. This is what Eckersley calls systemic optimism: a view that believes we need to change the underlying principles on which organisations and whole societies are based. Its view of the future is filled with a sense of impatience at the lack of dynamism and drive within the system, and a growing realisation that the way government and public agencies think about the world no longer corresponds to reality. It believes the central purpose of 'a viable global future' is, in Willis Harman's words, 'to advance human growth and development to the fullest extent [and] to promote human learning'.[4]

The three Scotlands are, of course, a simplification. In truth, people, communities and organisations move between the three, and sit in different places at different times and issues. But together they illustrate some of the key faultlines and tensions in Scotland, its cultures and institutions.

The limits of 'the official future'

The modernist perspective is 'the official future' of Scotland – the perspective offered by the main political, governing and institutional elites of the country. Peter Schwartz, the doyen of futures thinking, describes the official future thus:

> It stands for the set of implicit assumptions behind the most institutional policies – that things will work out okay tomorrow once the proper people get into power and can put their policies into effect.[5]

Most 'official futures' according to Schwartz turn out to be 'mere propaganda', and yet at the same time 'everybody in an organisation subscribes to them almost unconsciously . . . working towards an impossible or undesirable goal.'[6]

The 'official future' is based on a set of assumptions that have become unquestioned across the world: economic growth, consumption, competition and choice are good, and that we operate in a new economic and social paradigm where individuals have to look after themselves, not rely on others and certainly not on government. One of the main issues for this perspective in Scotland is improving economic growth, which has been lagging behind the rest of the UK for the last 35 years, and it has become the mainstream consensus that this is one of the main issues for government and policy-makers to address.

This mindset never acknowledges that for all Scotland's slow post-war growth in comparison to the rest of the UK, the last 35 years have seen Scottish GDP double in size, and on current trends it will double again before 2040. Is this really the Scotland we want to live in, and would this 'official future' actually bring us more happiness and contentment, or would more wealth, consumption, competition and inequality result in less happiness and a more mean country and culture? One of the major dialogues in this collection casts serious doubt on the link between economic growth and life satisfaction.[7]

This 'official future' invokes a world view which emphasises how powerless we all are in the face of huge global and societal forces and change. It invokes the Thatcherite mantra 'There Is No Alternative' to brush aside dissent or discontent. Despite its rhetoric of change, choice and opportunity, it contributes to a sense of widespread pessimism and fatalism about how much influence people can have on the future of their lives and societies.

The power and grip of this mantra in Scotland and across the Western world is directly linked to political disconnection and disillusion, because people feel they are not being valued or listened to. It is a powerful message to send out: the future has already been decided.

The 'official future' is the new grammar of politics – the language of choice for the governing classes. People use its language and phrases such as 'the knowledge economy', 'globalisation' and 'value added' often without defining, or understanding them. Many people feel they have little choice but to use these terms to gain access to the policy community and governing circles.

Scottish fatalism can be seen across a number of areas of society. It can be seen in the stories we tell each other. The historian Tom Devine has commented that many of the stories we use are frequently characterised by 'melancholic negativism' and 'introspective navel gazing'.[8] It can be seen in the country's appalling public health record and the degree of poverty and inequality in the most deprived communities in the country.

The most striking feature of public health and poverty in Scotland, apart from the scale, is the widespread acceptance of and resignation to it. For a country that prides itself on its egalitarian ethos and its belief that we are all 'Jock Tamson's Bairns', there is an ominous silence at the heart of Scottish public discourse about the scale of poverty and exclusion.

For Scotland to challenge the 'official story' it needs to embrace the idea of hope. Much public discourse in Western societies has seen the displacement of hope by cynicism and critique. However, hope is a vital virtue according to John Braithwaite, who argues that we need to institutionalise hope by supporting focusing adaptiveness and active coping, reducing denial and preventing disengagement.[9]

Thinking optimistically about Scotland's future is crucial, but it is not enough. Instead of linear optimism, we need systemic optimism. This is a clash of very different philosophies. Linear optimists inhabit the world of business and politics, talk about fine-tuning and trying to perfect institutions, and believe in material progress. Systemic optimists sit within and outwith the system, believe in whole-system change, instead of piecemeal reform, and advocate a more sustainable idea of progress. One is centred on the pursuit of individualism and the maximal self, the other on interconnectedness and a social self.

Systemic optimism has much in common with what the American psychologist Martin Seligman has called 'flexible' or 'learned optimism'. This recognises the complexities and different challenges we face. The power of pessimism can in certain circumstances be a force for good, such as when we face significant risk or a life-threatening situation, and 'learned optimism' combines this with the strength of 'optimism with its eyes open'.[10] The potential of hopeful Scotland is a mindset of learned and systemic optimism, whose recognition of the need for whole-system change is conducive to thinking differently about the future.

Don't stop thinking about tomorrow

The concept of 'futures literacy' is central to our argument that thinking about the future is not something that can be safely left to futurologists. Futures literacy, as described in a later chapter, helps us challenge our everyday assumptions and leads to better decision-making. To be futures literate means thinking imaginatively about the future but also to be able to act in the present.

That is why we have suggested that futures thinking should be a participative exercise that involves people across the whole of Scotland, rather than being confined to the powerful institutions that are usually asked to think about our future on our behalf. We see the development of futures literacy as a direct challenge to the fatalist streak in Scotland.

There is growing evidence that giving people a stake in the future encourages them to think long term and to make better decisions. The political argument in favour of developing asset holding makes the link between a stake in the future and better decision-making by individuals and communities. As Michael Sherraden, Director of the Center for Social Development at Washington University, has argued:

We say that people have assets when they accumulate and hold resources for the longer term. When this happens it has many positive effects for individuals and families (not merely deferred consumption). These positive effects include greater long-term thinking and planning for the future, increased participation in the community and investments in oneself, financial products, property, and enterprise for greater returns.[11]

We believe that asking people to think about their community as an asset in which they have a real stake and whose future needs to be secured has the potential to generate positive engagement. Scotland 2020 found evidence of this power in a public engagement experiment in Nairn, which is examined later. Involving the public in generating practical solutions to long-term community problems would require a greater capacity to think about the future, or futures literacy. As Zygmunt Bauman has argued, the idea of progress has always been about 'the self-confidence of the present'.[12]

Politicians across the Western world are always talking about the need for hard choices, but in reality only offer a narrow, proscriptive future. Citizens often seem to be ahead of politicians in thinking honestly about future prospects. The sense of disengagement from current institutions may be one manifestation of this. This offers some positive signs that the general public across the Western democracies may be open to futures literacy. But to express shared hopes and participate in collective solutions, people need shared institutions and processes.

Fundamental to this goal is developing a two-way conversation between voters and politicians. Recent exercises such as Labour's 'Big

Conversation' or the Conservatives' attempt to position themselves as 'the listening party' are unlikely to achieve very much. They are attempts to break political disillusion and the sense of 'them' and 'us', but they have both foundered on the prevailing dynamic of an enclosed, adversarial politics.

Genuine dialogue means shifting the balance from Hirschman's 'exit' – taking one's custom elsewhere – to 'voice' – the power of argument and persuasion.[13] This means giving citizens more options for expressing their views than switching or withholding their vote and instead exploring new ways for people to contribute to the way they are governed.

According to Peter Kellner, such politics requires a different kind of politician: 'Respect is deserved by those who know both when to lead and when to listen.' Kellner's prognosis for aiding this include allowing politicians to be more human and make mistakes and gaffes such as John Prescott's famous left hook in the 2001 election when he hit a voter who threw eggs at him. The alternative is 'politicians drained of humanity, humility, life and candour'.[14]

Such a politics has to be more local. We know from numerous social surveys that people relate national policies to their own experience. Yet at the same time, local services are consistently seen as good, whereas the same services at a national level are viewed as poor. It is quite common for people never to make the link between their own experience and national policy – whether it be in hospital, school, or Gordon Brown's Working Person's Tax Credit. Any realistic rebalancing of the central–local relationship will require a renewal of local capacity in local government and beyond, and a less centralised politics and media coverage.

A futures literate public would embrace the capacity to think and talk about the future, using a new language and grammar of politics. Developing a futures literate culture would be one that recognised that thinking about the future means embracing a world where there is uncertainty and unpredictability, and where there are many futures and many future Scotlands.

Nairn Day: futures thinking in a small Scottish town

Nairn Day was an experiment in local democracy that focused on participation rather than consultation (see chapter 20 for a detailed account). Nairn Day showed an appetite and indeed an aptitude for members of the public to think about the future of their community.

Communities often complain they are over-consulted. Their frustration may come from the feeling that they are being asked the wrong questions, or that the choices on offer do not allow for a discussion of the decisions already taken. A public consultation over where to site a new school may close down a debate about whether a new school is needed, or what kind of education parents want for their children.

Similarly, in hotly contested decisions to close local hospitals, the debate about the future of an institution becomes a poor substitute for wider discussion about public health. Local campaigns to overturn decisions about schools and hospitals often focus on inconvenience, but the anger that fuels them is a sense that decision-making processes are remote from the effects of the decisions that they take.

Nairn Day was an unusual exercise in that there was no agenda, beyond the encouragement to think about the future of the town and surrounding area. Participants were self-selecting, although we made some efforts to ensure diversity. We were encouraged to hear people say that it was not just the usual suspects who turned up.

The fact that over 70 people turned out to a meeting with no real agenda and certainly no influence over decision-making is, we think, evidence of an appetite for deliberation over long-term issues. This was not an expression of Nimbyism, but something more creative, imaginative and forward-looking.

There have been several experiments in linking public deliberation to local decision-making around the world. Perhaps one of the most famous of these is the participatory budget setting in Porto Alegre, Brazil. To combat decades of financial maladministration, where budgets were allocated on the basis of political patronage rather than social need, a new centre-left coalition government involved people directly, rather than through party representation, in the process of allocating municipal money.

In *Deepening Democracy*, Archon Fung and Erik Olin Wright consider four innovative democratic experiments, including that in Porto Alegre. They give examples of what they called empowered participatory governance, which they describe as an attempt 'to discover and imagine democratic institutions that are at once more participatory and effective than the familiar configuration of political representation and bureaucratic administration'.[15]

The key features of the form of governance that Fung and Olin Wright describe are that it:

o   focuses on real problems
o   involves ordinary people affected by those problems
o   helps to solve those problems through public deliberation.

What was striking about Nairn Day was that although the event was not designed to consider a specific problem faced by the town, the participants themselves steered the discussions towards practical issues such as transport and safer streets. The participants were comfortable talking the language of *priorities*, which underpins all public policy deliberations.

Futures thinking has two advantages to offer the process of public deliberation. First, creating the opportunity to think about the future of a community seems to motivate people to get involved. Second, greater futures literacy would develop the capacity to think constructively about future priorities.

We believe that the appetite for public participation displayed in Nairn, combined with examples of practical local problem-solving such as in Porto Alegre, suggests that further democratic experiments at local level could pay off at a time of widespread concern about political disengagement. Engaging people in local politics requires opportunity and motive. It is our view that opening up a public debate about the future of communities in the vicinity of elected politicians provides both.

A self-governing Scotland

The pre-devolution expectations of the Scottish public coalescing around the hope for a 'new politics' of consultation, participation and transparent process have not been delivered. The sense of disappointment and disillusion which pervades large parts of Scottish public discussion has become the new post-devolution consensus: a mindset of negativity that reinforces the Scots' propensity to face the same way, and ignores the complexity and diversity of any one moment.

Developing futures thinking could be a way to improve the quality of Scotland's political culture and engage people in a form of practical problem-solving within their community. The practice of futures thinking offers a way to tip the balance of local and national politics.

But that is not the way things are moving in Scotland. The creation of a new national political institution has drawn power to the centre in a number of ways: institutionally, in the way networks and groups think and operate around government, and in the media. So, perhaps inevitably, devolution from Westminster has meant the increasing concentration of power in Edinburgh, while to others in the more far-flung regions of the country, it appears that the Central Belt is where attention and power lies.

In this context, the now familiar form of 'localism', which encourages participation in the management of services, is misguided: it implies that communities should be involved in managerial decision-making, when really they should be involved in devising local strategies. To put it simply, communities should participate in devising public health strategies, not running hospitals; influencing the educational opportunities available to their children, not running schools; or helping to articulate an approach to community safety, not determining the number of police officers on the street.

Consultation on public services tends to occur at a stage where a decision has to be taken, but a lot of assumptions have already been made. Futures thinking offers a longer-term perspective so that issues can be considered while more options are open.

In the context of science policy, Demos has helped to develop the idea of 'upstream engagement' of the public in shaping the direction of scientific research and technological innovation. The decision over whether to allow genetically modified crops to be grown in Britain was the textbook example of downstream engagement according to James Wilsdon and Rebecca Willis: 'Possible risks [were] endlessly debated, while deeper questions about the values, vision and vested interests that motivate scientific endeavour often remain unasked or unanswered.'[16]

Any attempt to engage citizens in Scotland's future must take this lesson firmly to heart. Scottish politics often look like municipal administration writ large. Party loyalties are an entrenched feature of local politics, particularly in Labour's heartland of the west of Scotland. The paradox of Scottish political culture is that national government operates in a municipal fashion, while municipalities are ruled by parties whose ideological identity and support is largely based on their national profile.

However, there are welcome signs that vision might be emerging as a new dimension of Scottish political culture. George Reid, the Presiding Officer of the Scottish Parliament, has announced his aim to create a futures forum that would help to make Scotland a world leader in futures thinking. This admirable idea risks perpetuating the desire to find a single vision for Scotland, to define a single Scotland.

Reid has already indicated that he plans to reject the Finnish model of a parliamentary committee for the future. The Finnish committee is in effect a parliamentary think tank, with MPs taking evidence from a range of experts and delivering reports to the Parliament. We believe the futures forum should, as its defining characteristic, make a commitment from the centre to stimulate, support and resource widespread engagement in futures literacy among Scotland's communities. Instead of just thinking about this, it would practise a new kind of process which included the following elements:

○ a new kind of political centre – one that is enabling, facilitative and offers resources in a hands-off way; while the centre agrees to facilitate futures thinking, local governance should feed back deliberations to the centre

O   avoidance of the trap of posing futures thinking as some kind of received wisdom

O   support for multiple Scottish communities – perhaps starting geographically, but eventually including communities of interest

O   more empowered, emboldened, confident communities and a centre that is ready to evolve and adapt in response

O   a readiness to embrace and invent a new relationship between citizen and state, remaking the idea of government, governance and what 'governed' means.

This could have a huge impact on local communities. We believe exercises similar to Nairn Day should be encouraged as part of the local authority electoral cycle. A programme of local futures activities conducted ahead of the four-yearly council elections would encourage an articulation of a vision for an area by both voters and politicians. We believe such processes should encourage involvement by insiders and outsiders, and involve artists, ideas people, imagineers and other storytellers who can assist in developing different ways of telling the stories of the future.

Developing futures thinking capacity at a local level could have a number of advantages and spin-offs. It would be a symbolic commitment, which also helped to improve the context – the climate of conversation – in which political decisions are taken. It could begin a process of genuine democratisation and self-government across Scotland, which goes far beyond political structures, helping to refresh local governance and deepen the pool of talent feeding our representative institutions.

The long-term goal is a different, more mature public leadership and public conversation. This in turn could strengthen a prefigurative politics for a future Scotland – one that is a decentralised, self-governing group of communities and networks maintaining a shared responsibility for an open, and hopeful, future. Such a strategy will take time, patience and learning. We believe it is worth the effort.

Gerry Hassan is a Demos associate and Eddie Gibb is head of external relations at Demos. They jointly lead the Scotland 2020 project.

Notes

1   J Frank, 'The role of hope in psychotherapy', *International Journal of Psychotherapy* 5, no 5 (1968): p 393.

2   G Mulgan, 'Essentials of change', speech to Joseph Rowntree Foundation centenary conference Poverty and Place: policies for tomorrow, 2004 (available at: www.jrf.org.uk/conferences/centenary/pdf/essentialsofchange.pdf).

3   R Eckersley, *Well and Good: how we feel and why it matters* (Melbourne: The Text Publishing Group, 2004), p 18.

4   W Harman, 'Global dimensions and the plausibility of whole system change', *Technological and Social Change* 49 no 1 (1995): p 10.

5   P Schwartz, *The Art of the Long View: planning for the future in an uncertain world* (London: Doubleday, 1996), p 203.

6   Ibid, p 203.

7   For a further examination of this argument see D Bell and DG Blanchflower, *The Scots may be Brave but they are neither Healthy nor Happy* (Stirling: Scotecon, 2004).

8   T Devine, speech to Scotland's Tipping Point conference, Glasgow, 2 December 2004, quoted in A Young, 'A sigh of relief, the apocalypse has been postponed until 2017', *Herald*, 10 Dec 2004.

9   J Braithwaite, 'Hope and emancipation', paper for Hope and Governance seminar series, 2003 (available at: http://regnet.anu.edu.au/research/Hope_Gov/Hope_Gov.htm).

10 MEP Seligman, *Learned Optimism: how to change your mind and your life* (New York: A A Knopf, 1991).

11 M Sherraden, in W Paxton (ed), *Equal Shares? Building a progressive and coherent asset-based welfare policy* (London: IPPR, 2003).

12 Z Bauman, *The Individualized Society* (London: Polity Press, 2001), p 110.

13 A Hirschman, *Exit, Voice and Loyalty: responses to decline in firms, organisations and states* (Cambridge: Harvard University Press, 1970).

14 P Kellner, 'Britain's culture of detachment', *Parliamentary Affairs* 54 no 4 (2004): pp 840, 841.

15 A Fung and E Olin Wright, *Deepening Democracy* (London: Verso, 2003).

16 J Wilsdon and R Willis, *See-through Science: why public engagement needs to move upstream* (London: Demos, 2004).

2. That was Then and This is Now

Imagining new stories about a northern nation

Gerry Hassan

Scotland has changed in the last 20 years. It has been transformed economically, socially, culturally and politically. It has a degree of self-government and a new set of political institutions. However, the way we think of and describe Scotland has not undergone a similar change; instead it is still rooted in a romanticised rose-tinted view of a past Scotland that is now long since gone.

This chapter looks at the extent of change in Scotland over this period and the kind of changes which may occur in the future. It argues that the idea of story and storytelling is a rich and illuminating way to understand Scotland. The stories we Scots tell each other, that we choose to believe and not to believe, help to create our collective mindset. And crucial to far-reaching change in Scotland is the need for a new story.

Scotland 1981 and the 'Quiet Revolution'

The Scotland of over 20 years ago was a nation already shaped by its past: a male manufacturing sector (even then, at only 24 per cent of the workforce), a trade union culture (at over 50 per cent of the workforce) and council housing (52 per cent of households). This was also an age of mass unemployment, significant economic and social dislocation and political disempowerment associated with a Tory government most Scots did not vote for. In short, these were not happy times, but an age filled with anger, hurt and bruised lives.

What was even more marked was the geographic distribution of this Scotland, particularly in relation to housing. In 1981, 40 of Scotland's 71 constituencies had over 50 per cent council housing, with a whole swathe of parliamentary seats in the west of Scotland having 70 per cent or plus council housing and very little owner occupation. The top two seats, Glasgow Provan and Garscadden, had 96 per cent and 90 per cent council housing, respectively, and these Stalinist proportions of public housing defined many of the cities and communities, and aided a kind of social apartheid across large parts of Scotland.

Ten years later, after a decade of Thatcherism and council house sales, a dramatic change had occurred, with only 14 of 72 seats having over 50 per cent council housing, with the top ten even more con-centrated in Glasgow. The top two, Airdrie and Shotts, and Mother-well and Wishaw, both had 62.5 per cent council housing.

Fast forwarding another decade to 2001, and not one of the 72 seats had over 50 per cent council housing. With the top two seats remaining the same as ten years previously – Motherwell and Wishaw, and Airdrie and Shotts – their proportions fell dramatically to 37.2 per cent and 36.2 per cent, respectively.[1]

This transformation of how Scots live has had profound consequences for society at many of levels: from the social layout and feel of cities, to the way young people think about their aspirations, future prospects and saving patterns, to newspaper supplements and TV programmes on this related domestic revolution, and the number of DIY and garden centres.

Across a range of other areas Scotland has undergone similar change – trade unionism has become a minority pastime of tenured public sector professionals, manufacturing has fallen from 24 per cent of the workforce to a mere 12 per cent (the same as financial services), and Scotland has become a service sector economy, if not culture. The economy has changed from one with high levels of official, visible unemployment to one with a significantly lower rate of official unemployment, a relatively high economic activity rate,[2] but deepening and embedded degrees of exclusion from the labour market for large sections of the adult population. And 20 years ago the power of social conservatism had a claustrophobic hold on Scottish public and elite opinion. The liberal reforms of the 1960s, and in particular abortion and homosexuality, were not discussed in public, whereas today the secularisation and liberalisation of Scotland is slowly bringing these issues into the open.

These changes are similar to the broad thrust of economic and social change across the Western world, but what has been different in Scotland has been the scale and speed of change. These amount to a profound shift towards:

O a more individualised society shaped in action and behaviour by lifestyle and consumer issues, and conspicuous consumption

O a society more at ease with issues of equality such as racism, sectarianism and homosexuality, although progress still remains to be made in all of these

O a society that was shaped in its culture by a deeply masculinised ethos in work, public life and politics, but which has become increasingly feminised with more women in work, public life and politics (with 40 per cent of the Scottish Parliament made up of women MSPs)

O a politics which is increasingly post-labourist – moving beyond the politics of clientism associated with the Labour local state, but which is also distinctly post-nationalist – transcending old-fashioned ideas of sovereignty.

Scotland has changed fundamentally in the last 20 years, but what is revealing is that this change has not been felt across every area of life. One part of Scottish society has remained immune, and that is how we think, describe and understand the country we live in. The mindset, the stories and narratives of Scotland have not changed along with the ways individual citizens lead their daily lives.

The dominant public discourses of Scotland still encapsulate a hankering after a world that has long since past, one that was dying and declining even 20 years ago. There is a romanticised nostalgia for collectivism and the uplifting hand it gave working-class families generations ago, without remembering the suffocating embrace it also had. The attraction of this remembered collectivism can be seen across culture and politics. It can be found in the urban kailyard novels of William McIlvanney and James Kelman which speak to the lost male world of the 'walking wounded'; and in the media with the McLad phenomenon of commentators such as Tam Cowan and Stuart Cosgrove, where middle-class men parade their working-class credentials. Politically, it is seen in the way Tommy Sheridan's Scottish Socialist Party[3] is given sympathetic and uncritical coverage in the press because it invokes a collectivist memory that all Scots have grown up with and which feels familiar.

There is illuminating survey evidence to support this sense that how Scots think about their country has not changed over the last 20 years. The Scottish Election Survey of 1979 and the Scottish Social Attitudes survey of 1999 on self-perceived class backs this up. First, overall, Scots think of themselves as slightly more working class in 1999 compared with 1979. Second, even the Scots professional and managerial group, who felt themselves more middle class than working class in 1979, now see themselves by a majority as working class. Scotland now sees itself as such a working-class country, that every socioeconomic group (using Goldthorpe's six social groups) identifies as such.

It is true that the meaning of class, 'working class' and 'middle class' does not remain static through the years, but is constantly being reshaped, renegotiated and reinterpreted. However, it is surely significant that in a period when Scotland has become more professional, and the overall size of its manual working class has shrunk dramatically, Scots respondents have shifted in the other direction. What seems to have happened is that the identification of a section of the professional classes with opposition to Thatcherism post-1979 has contributed to a section of this group continuing to identify as working class. In a very different experience from England post-1979, upward mobility in Scotland has not become synonymous with middle-class aspirations. Eighty per cent of working-class respondents (on Goldthorpe's criterion) who were upwardly mobile into the middle class still think of themselves as working class.[4]

Towards 2020

What Scotland requires is an ethic of living – a set of stories or narratives – that embodies and reflects the ways we live our lives. This cannot be the old social democracy or nationalist sentiments, which no longer explain contemporary realities. It has to capture the more individualist, pluralist and complex society – a society which has experienced similar economic and social change to other Western societies, but at a faster pace – while also embracing and celebrating a sense of distinctiveness which relates to Scottish identities and cultures.

Whatever forces become the champions and advocates of this emergent Scotland have a historic opportunity. In the political realm, they could win a dividend which could shape Scottish society and politics for over a generation – in the way people thought the Tories might have done in the 1950s, Labour did from the 1960s onwards, and the SNP have threatened at points since. Championing the new Scotland would entail:

o   being more individualist in some areas – accepting some of the philosophy of the 1980s Thatcherite agenda
o   rethinking some of Scotland's collectivist traditions without abandoning all of them – renewing some of the best of Labour's values
o   embracing a politics comfortable with a nationalist dimension – and which a post-nationalist SNP would be part of.

In the last two centuries Scotland has passed through different phases of progressive politics, which have defined a large part of the political consensus of the country:

○ Nineteenth-century Scotland was shaped by the values of the Gladstonian Liberal Party – nonconformist, temperance, land reform – and the power and patronage of the Kirk which lasted well into the early twentieth century.

○ Twentieth-century Scotland from the 1920s onward has been influenced by a Labour Scotland which inherited some of the Liberal values such as a commitment to home rule, and added a collectivism institutionalised in the public sector, local government and education.

○ A third progressive moment is now upon us – one which cannot be produced and socialised in hierarchical institutions, but will have to be made and remade by the consent and active engagement of the Scottish people themselves.

This third age will be more diffuse, fluid and difficult to categorise or control. The old top-down ways of patronage and professional elites which have for so long characterised contemporary Scotland have long outlived their use. They increasingly do not fit the world of complexity and change we live in, and this creates a unique opportunity for the Scots to shape a new kind of progressive settlement based on the language, relationships and interactions of people themselves.

The power of storytelling

One of the most important ways in which we understand the world is through the idea of stories. This has become increasingly recognised across different areas of life: business, politics, media and other avenues which rely on the power of persuasion and communication. Robert McKee, writer, director and lecturer on screenwriting, argues that 'our appetite for story' is:

> . . . a reflection of the profound human need to grasp the patterns of living, not merely as an intellectual exercise, but within a very personal, emotional experience.[5]

The storyteller invents a story, according to McKee, by asking a number of key questions:

> First, what does my protagonist want in order to restore balance in his or her life? Desire is the blood of a story. Desire is not a shopping list but a core need. . . . Next, what is keeping my protagonist from achieving his or her desire? Forces within? Doubt? Fear? Confusion? Personal conflicts with friends, family, lovers? Social conflicts arising in the various institutions in society?[6]

The next stage involves asking 'how would my protagonist decide to act in order to achieve his or her desire in the face of these antagonistic forces?' And, in the answer to this question we find, in McKee's words, 'the truth of their characters because of the choices he or she makes under pressure'. The final storytelling phase involves reflecting on 'the design of events' and asking, 'Do I believe this?'[7]

McKee believes 'self-knowledge is the root of all great storytelling', and this has been substantiated by Christopher Booker's magisterial tour de force on the importance of stories and why they matter so much to us. Booker answers the question of 'why certain images, symbols and shaping forms recur in stories' with the observation:

> We must first look to those deeper levels of unconscious which we all have in common, as part of our basic genetic inheritance. These work around what Jung called 'archetypes': 'the ancient river beds along which our psychic current naturally flows'.[8]

Howard Gardner, in his ambitious and wide-ranging study of leadership, identifies one of the main characteristics of leaders as the ability to tell stories which define the age or point in history we live in. At any given date – 1940 or 1979 in Britain, 1940–41 and 1980 in the United States – there are a multiplicity of stories and counter-stories in circulation, and the successful stories: Churchill's 'finest hour', Thatcher's counter-revolution, resonate at the time, and define it for years to come. According to Gardner:

> . . . *most of the stories that leaders tell are created in response to the pervasive human need to understand better oneself, the groups that exist in and beyond one's culture, and issues of value and meaning. Indeed, stories in the broadest sense – narratives, visions, dreams, embodiments – are most effective when they provide at the same time nourishment for the mind (or the understanding), on the one hand, and a feeling of belonging and security, on the other.*[9]

When screenwriters do not know how to end a story, they resort to one of a number of tried and tested clichés. The same is true of politicians. According to McKee:

> *As they reach into their minds for material, they come up empty. . . . From the works of other writers they crib scenes we've seen before, paraphrase dialogue we've heard before, disguise characters we've met before, and pass them off as their own.*[10]

And this is true of recent examples of British leaders. Thatcher's story of reversing British economic decline ran into the ground after her enemies had been slayed: trade unions and nationalised industries. Following Thatcherism's high point, the Tories failed to offer a new story, and descended into infighting, sleaze and being seen as out of touch. Tony Blair's story of modernising the party and the slogan 'New Labour, New Britain' have come unstuck as Labour failed to transform public services and invent a new credo of social democracy. Blair's support for George W Bush and the Iraq war has come at the worst point for Blair's story – as it is beginning to unravel and failing to find a new narrative.[11]

Scottish Stories: the eleven basic stories of Scottish history

Scotland is a land rich in history, myth, folklore and, of course, stories.[12] According to McCrone, Scotland 'is a landscape of the mind, a place of imagination'.[13] As a 'nation' it is both 'imagined' and a 'community', in Benedict Anderson's words, giving a sense of place and time.[14] A recent fascinating narrative of the nation was provided by Frank Delaney's *Ireland: a novel*, where through the use of storytelling he has framed the history of the country: 'this is a country that processes itself through the mills of its imagination'.[15]

A number of defining stories can be seen through the last 300 years of Scotland since the Treaty of Union:

o   **Enterprising Scotland** – this is the land of engineers, inventors and imagineers: a nation which built bridges, railways and roads across the world. This is a rich territory which offers some of the most powerful archetypal Scots role models through the generations, such as Scotty, the engineer in the *Star Trek* TV series.

o   **Empire Scotland** – this is the Victorian and post-Victorian ideal of warrior Scotland, whereby Scottish regiments fought across the world for empire, imperialism and colonialism. This tradition exists to this day – as Scotland continues to play a crucial role in the post-empire imperial tradition – in Iraq and elsewhere.

o   **Enlightenment Scotland** – this is the Scotland of learned debate, intellectual enquiry, rationalism, and a belief in the power of ideas, logic and science. This is a Scotland connected to Unionist and Empire Scotland, inspired to understand the universe, but so nervous about its Scottishness that it tried to eradicate it.

o   **Educational Scotland** – the importance of the democratic intellect, the lad o' pairts, the Kirriemuir career and so on. These add up to a belief that Scots education is part of an egalitarian Scotland where people from the most humble background get on.

○ **Calvinist Scotland** – the nation as God's chosen country, shaped by the theocracy of the Reformation which has percolated down through the years, and can still be seen today in the Scots' sense of unease about sex, the body and emotions.

○ **Tartan Scotland** – the world of kilts, heather and tartan dress and symbols, and the Highlands as romantic, defiant and ultimately defeated. This is a problematic iconic story – used to sell Scotland to the world, but filled with ambiguity and a sense of unease about the history invested in it, and its relation to modern Scotland.

○ **Kailyard Scotland** – an idealised backward rural society set in the nineteenth century based on a longing for the virtues of small town Scotland against urban industrialisation. In the twentieth century this was articulated by among others DC Thomson publishers and the *Sunday Post* newspaper.

○ **Divided Scotland** – this is the land of the divided self seen in Dr Jekyll and Mr Hyde, RD Laing and, more recently, Tom Nairn's studies of Scots identity. This is a nation split between Highland and Lowland, Catholic and Protestant, heart and mind, euphoria and self-doubt, which pathologises itself into believing it has a schizophrenic dual identity.

○ **Collectivist Scotland** – this is the progressive Scotland which gave birth to Labour's institutional dominance of Scotland for most of the twentieth century. An alternative version of this story is dependency culture Scotland – the Thatcherite explanation for Scotland's resistance to its charms, which has more recently been adopted by Blairite New Labour.

○ **Unionist Scotland** – this stresses the benefits of the Union, and in its modern version emphasises the degree to which Scotland is subsidised by the rest of the UK. It also still draws on an older argument, questioning the capacity of Scots to govern themselves.

O **Nationalist Scotland** – this rests on the 'Scotland Why Not?' argument which is centred on the premise that Scotland is a nation, therefore it follows logically it should be independent. Another more apolitical nationalism can be found across the political spectrum. As Scottish identity has become more pronounced it has celebrated a negative story – of who we are not, ie: 'we're not English', and a sense of anti-Englishness.

Over the last 300 years there has been a profound degree of contesting, conflict and contradiction, both between and within stories. None of the above stories are entirely harmonious, clear cut, linear narratives, but contain within them, disparate and sometimes disputatious forces, such as the argument within Unionist Scotland over whether to identify more with the British state, defend Scottish distinctiveness, or support a Scottish Parliament in the UK.

Post-devolution stories

Moving to the experience of Scotland since the establishment of the Parliament in May 1999, the post-devolution environment has been shaped by a series of stories:

O **The Holyrood Building Project** – the story of how the construction of the Scottish Parliament went from £40 million to £431 million. This is a world where politicians and civil servants are seen as either corrupt, self-serving, incompetent, or all three.

O **The Toytown Parliament story** – a view held by fundamentalist Nationalists ('Scotland free or a desert') which believes that Holyrood is toothless as well as spineless, and not worthy of the word Parliament. Elements of Old Labour hold a similar view because they believe constitutional change is a diversion from class politics.

O **The Souped-up Labour Cooncil** – this sees the Parliament as the revenge of Lanarkshire Man (and it is Man) and as nothing but a super-remunerated town council, offering jobs for the boys, and run by Labour 'numpties' (meaning a certain kind of councillor).

O **Politically correct Scotland** – this is the perception of certain, very vocal, right-wing elements of the press. Section 28, the ban on foxhunting, and the forthcoming ban on smoking in public spaces are all used to give support to the Scots 'nanny state' argument.

The Holyrood Building Project in particular became the most potent story of the last few years in Scotland. It has become the 'taxi driver' story of contemporary Scotland – a story that has gained power by its repeated telling and retelling allowing it to pass into folklore and myth, and which has gained currency by its simplicity and black and white clarity. What unites all of the above stories is that they are negative accounts of the early years of Scotland's Parliament; they diminish the degree of change which has come about and undermine the capacity of people to believe they can bring about change.

The missing element in these crucial years has been any positive account: an absence which goes to the heart of the sense of public disillusionment and disconnection which a large number of Scottish citizens feel about devolution. This has fed into a widespread sense that campaigners expended much energy on getting a Parliament, and fine-tuning the institutional arrangements without putting a great deal of thought into what the new institution would actually do, what purpose it would serve, and what kind of Scotland it would advance.[16]

If we are to aid, support and encourage change in Scotland, we have to identify and nurture a sense of story. Such stories need to acknowledge, as Gardner does, the crucial role of leadership. In an age of mass media, where there is less deference and respect for tradition and authority, leadership has to reflect this. It is the more old-fashioned forms of authority which are still most prevalent throughout Scotland – institutionally based and shaped by formal notions of mission and mandate. These forms will continue to be important and have their place, but they must be supplemented by new forms which are more flexible and more rooted for legitimacy in communication, consent and creating alliances. Some commentators have talked of the rise of 'postmodern leadership' across the Western world, but the problem with this concept is that the leaders who have so far been identified with it – Clinton and Blair – have had decidedly mixed records.[17] Politics founded on individual trust and charisma, politics as personality, has all kinds of pitfalls, as the decline of Tony Blair post-Iraq war shows, but politics based exclusively on institutional mandates is just as problematic.

Related to the idea of leadership is the nature of the relationships we can have in public life, and how we can build honest, open and creative forms of dialogue. One crucial factor here is the dominance of institutional opinion, which is well organised, funded and has access to the channels of power. Given the Scots' historic creation of consensus for a variety of reasons, this contributes to a constraining of debate. Encouraging more constructive and open dialogue involves a range of steps, which can begin with creating and identifying new spaces and forums whereby innovative processes of engagement are used to allow a more honest, reflective form of dialogue. At an ultimate level, the Scots' propensity to consensus and sitting in the 'big tent' facing the same way has to be challenged, and the fear of disagreement removed.

Vital to all of the above is the idea of progress. In the mid-twentieth century the Scottish dream of progress was a socialist one. With the death of the collectivist ideal, Scotland lost a sense of certainty and mission. In the late twentieth century, another utopian ideal came along promising total fulfilment and freedom of a very different kind: one based on individualised, marketised relationships. Contemporary Scotland seems to be caught between these two world views and utopias: on the one hand harking back to its previous era of progress, and being unable to let go of it, while, in the daily acts of individuals, living in this new age of anomie and consumption. A number of stories are on offer for a future Scotland:

O **Labour minimalist devolution** – Labour holds on to its position as the leading party of Scottish politics despite the challenge of a more pluralist politics. It manages to restrain the potential of politics and the new institutions, and thus a minimalist devolution is characterised by the politics of continuity, rather than change.

O **Post-nationalist Scotland** – the SNP explicitly abandons the idea of old-fashioned nationalism, and embraces a politics of shared sovereignty, governing in a devolved Scotland, and challenging Labour's ossified version of social democracy, as well as its role as the nation's leading party.

O **Black and white Scotland** – this is the continuation of contemporary Scotland along the lines we have seen in the early years of devolution. This would continue to question the Scots' ability to govern themselves, and encourage a blame and betrayal culture where cynicism and disillusionment are the norm. This is a self-perpetuating cycle which will bring about the doom and gloom thesis it is railing against.

O **Smart Scotland** – a marketised Scotland where the country is driven by the dynamics and logic of 'the knowledge economy', upskilling and egovernance. This Smart Scotland is a country fearlessly embracing change and flexibility, opening itself to globalisation and the international market, and aspiring – as everyone does – to be the new Finland.

O **Adaptive Scotland** – a personalised Scotland of learning and listening, and evolving government, organisations and public agencies. Radical, innovative forms of public service emerge which are flexible, cross-cutting and

championed by new practices of working, collaboration
and leadership.

○ **New progressive Scotland** – this story embraces thematic
ways of understanding Scotland and promotes a confident
Scotland and the need for widespread cultural change. It
stresses that for too long the Scots have put the emphasis
on politics and politicians as the means of how to change
the world. Instead of conventional programmatic
methods, it emphasises health, well-being, status, self-
worth and other subjective indicators.

Any future Scotland will see a multiplicity of stories emerge, interact
and influence each other. A number of these stories are about limited
or blocking change (Labour minimalist, black and white Scotland),
while the rest are about different degrees and types of change (Post-
nat, Smart, Adaptive and New Prog). Leaving aside for the moment
the overtly political story of change – Post-nationalism – Smart
Scotland has attractions in its moves forward from the old social
democracy and collectivist past, but it has significant drawbacks, in its
technocratic, managerial, top-down and unquestioning assumptions
such as 'the knowledge economy' and 'globalisation'.

This leaves the potential of Adaptive Scotland – a story about
government, leadership and learning, which does not unquestioningly buy into any assumptions, but is based on evolving and
adapting as circumstances and challenges arise. It does, however,
contain elements of managerialism, and thus to develop
transformative change which is not top-down it could collaborate
with the New Progressive Scotland story. This view attempts to
develop a thematic approach, involve wider currents and opinion in
cultural change, and develop institutional and non-institutional
alliances.

Four strands of a future Scotland

A culture and society that aims to embrace radical change has to
develop a public conversation on a number of levels:

○ **A sense of story** – This means a sense of all-encompassing shared national purpose, cohesion and narrative that goes beyond advertising or branding. Several small countries across the world – Estonia, Finland, Ireland – seem to have this national purpose, and this is related to them having had a wide-ranging debate about the future of the country and the priorities that should be invested in. In an age of interdependence, it is not surprising that small countries might be more adept internally and externally at this, and also no accident that all three of them are formally independent.

○ **The power and resonance of song** – In the 1980s the musical backdrop to opposing Thatcherism was provided by the Proclaimers whose song 'Why do you let someone rule your land cap in hand' seemed to give articulation to the anger and sense of victimhood which characterised Scotland at the time. Post-devolution Scotland's song has, if anything, shifted to Travis, with their bland, middle of the road, inoffensive pop. A new song for a future Scotland might already be on offer, strangely, from the Proclaimers, who have moved from political proselytising to personal reflection as they have grown up. Craig and Charlie Reid, the twin brothers who make up the band, now sing on their latest album, *Born Innocent*, songs about growing up, bringing up your children, being a role model to them, and issues of emotional literacy. This seems to cover some of the central themes of any manifesto for a future Scotland, and better than most politicians could.

○ **Heroes** – In the words of the great Brian Wilson (musical genius and ex-leader of the Beach Boys), we need heroes as well as villains. Scotland seems to have plenty of villains – the taxi driver account of the Holyrood Building Project providing an entire political class to some – and a huge number of dead heroes – Wallace, Bruce, Burns et al. The idea of heroes may be devalued somewhat in our celebrity-obsessed culture,[18] but what we need are a few live heroes, and a public culture which allows us to celebrate and honour people and their achievements.

O **Honest public relationships** – This is perhaps the most basic and the most fundamental of all the shifts we need to make, and it involves being honest with each other, and having a sense of integrity and self-worth in the relationships and interactions we have. And this is about the kind of public culture, space and conversation we want to encourage.

All of the above involve making a significant shift in the mindset of mainstream Scotland, but the first steps have already been made. A large and growing element of Scotland, within and without institutional opinion, knows we need to do things differently and the old ways no longer suffice. This emerging force is not organised at the moment, but even within the heart of the institutions and interest groups of the country, there is a gathering sense by many that we need to change direction. Beginning this process of change can start on numerous different levels from the serious to the subtle, from the sublime to the ridiculous. It has already begun in debates in Scottish culture and history, where the Scots' propensity to look back and try and undo the past has undergone extensive scrutiny and examination. A recent example is the debate on Scotland's role in empire and colonialism.[19] Another positive sign of change is the emerging movement of opinion which believes that programmatic change in the form of legislation and formal political processes is not the best way of aiding change. Instead, across a range of areas – education, health, the wider public sector – a number of people are now advocating that we look at more diffuse issues such as culture, attitudes and values.

It is also about the kind of men and women we want to be, the kind of relationships we want to have with each other, and how we choose to bring up and love our children, and encourage them to be questioning, confident, caring individuals. And if we want to grow and learn from each other, developing conversations which are informed by emotional literacy, then we need to throw off the negative legacy of Calvinism. Scots men have to stop using football as an emotional substitute and displacement from connecting with one other. They have to realise, which should not be too difficult given the state of the game in Scotland, that it is, after all, only a sport.

Scotland then is on the verge of a new story. The example of small nations across the European Union such as Estonia, Finland and Ireland gives room for confidence, but also raises the difficult issue of independence. To some unionist politicians independence has played no part in the Irish Celtic Tiger. However, it is also true that independence on its own – the traditional Nationalist argument – does not automatically bring about national renewal. The Irish example is salutary here – formally independent since 1921, the Celtic Tiger success story took until the 1980s. Therefore, we can conclude that a nationalist narrative and independence may be important, but other factors – and the emergence of other, supportive stories – are equally vital.

Another factor in Scotland's future is its role in the multi-national, multi-identity, hybrid entity that is the United Kingdom. The moment of hope, post-1997, of Blairite New Labour, has long extinguished itself, and we are faced with the grim reality of a government which has embarked on an unprecedented degree of constitutional reform, without changing the relationships which make up the UK, or the mindset of the central state, where the political class, civil service and media still cling to the idea of the unitary state. As Scots brought up on the Treaty of Union ('two equals') know well, the UK was never a unitary state, but a union state, which allowed for Scottish distinctive arrangements. However, the centre has always misunderstood the UK as a unitary state, and still does.

This sense of the unreformed centre is crucial because of what the UK is. We live in a state which, despite being post-empire, is still shaped by post-imperial ideals of grandeur, the warrior state tradition, and the dependency of the British political classes on the so-called 'special relationship' with the US.[20] This, of course, has all come to a crucial juncture with Blairite New Labour's grotesque metamorphosis into a gunboat diplomacy version of liberal imperialism – sailing along side by side George W Bush's neo-con view of the world.

This all matters to Scotland, because part of its tradition and society has happily embraced empire, and to this day plays a crucial role in the British warrior state, while also finding itself constrained by the culture, codes and practice of the *ancien regime*. And it is always the case with the Scottish situation that any new movement of change and story which upsets the conventional order carries with it the potential of effecting much wider change across the British polity, which will benefit progressive opinion across the rest of the United Kingdom. A new Scottish story carries with it the potential of carrying its ripples and waves far beyond the boundaries and shores of this small northern nation. It could articulate a new narrative which brings change to Scotland, aid a far-reaching British trans-formation, and have wider lessons and implications across the world, not least for comparable small nations and territories.

Gerry Hassan is joint leader of the Scotland 2020 programme.

Notes

1   G Hassan and D Fraser, *The Political Guide to Modern Scotland: people, places and power* (London: Politico Publishing, 2004).

2   The Scottish rate at the end of 2004 – 75.1 per cent compared with a UK rate of 74.7 per cent – for the first time higher than the UK rate.

3   Tommy Sheridan stood down as the leader of the Scottish Socialist Party in November 2004, but to all practical intents and purposes no matter who the leader of the SSP is it will for the foreseeable future remain Tommy Sheridan's party.

4   L Paterson, F Bechhofer and D McCrone, *Living in Scotland: social and economic change since 1980* (Edinburgh: Edinburgh University Press, 2004), p 99.

5   R McKee, *Story: substance, structure, style and the principles of screenwriting* (London: Harper Collins, 1997), p 12.

6   R McKee, 'Storytelling that moves people', *Harvard Business Review*, June (2003), at p 8.

7 Ibid, p 8.

8 C Booker, *The Seven Basic Plots: why we tell stories* (London: Continuum, 2004), p 12.

9 H Gardner, *Leading Minds: an anatomy of leadership* (London: Harper Collins, 1996), p 50.

10 McKee, *Story*, pp 67–8.

11 D Finkelstein, 'Blair's story is coming to an end', *The Times*, 18 May 2004, p 3.

12 D Smith, *Storytelling Scotland: a nation in narrative* (Edinburgh: Polygon, 2001).

13 D McCrone, *Understanding Scotland: the sociology of a stateless nation* (London: Routledge, 1992), p 17.

14 B Anderson, *Imagined Communities: reflections on the origin and spread of nationalism* (London: Verso, 1983).

15 See author's note in F Delaney, *Ireland: a novel* (London: Time Warner, 2004).

16 G Hassan and C Warhurst, 'Future Scotland: the making of the New Social Democracy' in G Hassan and C Warhurst (eds), *Tomorrow's Scotland* (London: Lawrence and Wishart, 2002), pp 5–25.

17 S Schier (ed), *The Postmodern Presidency: Bill Clinton's legacy in US politics* (Pittsburgh: University of Pittsburgh Press, 2000).

18 L Hughes-Hallett, *Heroes: saviours, traitors and supermen* (London: Fourth Estate, 2004).

19 T Devine, *Scotland's Empire 1600–1815* (London: Allen Lane, 2004).

20 M Gardiner, *The Cultural Roots of British Devolution* (Edinburgh: Edinburgh University Press, 2004).

New narratives for a northern nation

Thinking about the future requires creativity. Analysing trends is not enough, however good the data. Imagining the future is an empowering process that opens up the possibility of action. These short stories by leading Scottish writers, which were inspired by a series of scenario-building workshops in Edinburgh, are intended to help us think differently about the future.

3. A Futures Literate Nation

Matthew Horne and Helen McCarthy

Developing 'futures literacy' in organisations improves decision-making and helps people prepare for an uncertain future. The challenge for Scotland is to become a futures literate nation.

As part of Scotland 2020, Demos ran two scenario-building workshops with diverse groups of people drawn from Scottish public life, including business leaders, senior public sector managers, academics and NGO campaigners. The day-long workshops were facilitated using a futures tool called FutureSight, which is described below.

As with many futures methodologies, the main outputs are scenarios, or stories about the future. Peter Schwartz likens scenarios to screenplays, with the drama emerging from the interaction between long-term trends. Given the importance of stories and narrative in this approach to scenario-building, we decided to involve Scottish writers in the workshops.

Their stories, which are published in this book, were inspired by their participation in the workshops and are not intended as faithful reports of the proceedings. These are clearly not the kind of scenarios on which large organisations would base their strategy. Instead they are an accessible way to help people think differently about the future. In short, they are intended as a tool to help develop Scotland's 'futures literacy'.

What is futures literacy?

None of us can escape having an opinion about what we think the future *will* be and what we think it *ought* to be. We are interested parties. Equally, none of the images of the future we produce are ever entirely 'right', or indeed entirely 'wrong'. No one can predict the future (although some, as we will see below, do try). It is, by its very nature, open and unknown. This is why it makes better sense to talk about possible *'futures'*, rather than *'the future'*.

We will never hold in our hands the crystal ball that can unlock the secrets of tomorrow. Nonetheless thinking about the future in a disciplined and structured way *can* be a constructive and valuable activity. Primarily it will help you make better decisions in the present, mindful of the full range of possibilities that the future might hold.

Individuals have the power to shape their environments effectively and responsibly, but too often are paralysed with fear about how to manage change. By considering a range of alternative futures in a safe but challenging space, we can get ourselves 'unstuck' from the assumptions we hold about the present.

This process of opening our minds to new possibilities is at the heart of what it means to be futures literate. The purpose of futures literacy is to:

o   reveal and challenge the assumptions we hold
o   make explicit our shared values
o   enable action now
o   create more robust decision-making in the present
o   discipline forward thinking
o   enable richer dialogue with colleagues and partners
o   become agents of change.

About FutureSight

Demos developed its Serious Futures methodology in the mid 1990s as a tool for developing policy ideas in such a way as to recognise that the environment in which policies are introduced is typically very different from the one in which they are devised. Serious Futures uses a scenario-building process to identify the risks, constraints and opportunities with which policy-makers have to contend, and to help them work with longer-term horizons.

More recently we have been working with the National College for School Leadership (NCSL),[1] which has developed its own distinctive approach to futures thinking contained in a group facilitation process called FutureSight. NCSL uses its concepts and techniques to create professional development experiences for school leaders, and Demos has used this methodology to develop futures literacy with a range of policy-makers and professions.

Futures literacy is about developing the capacity to inhabit a number of alternative possible futures. This means more than simple forward thinking. NCSL's FutureSight toolkit takes its name from the academic Hedley Beare, who describes this distinction thus:

> Merlin, the legends agree, could speak the language of trees and animals; he could communicate with birds and the creatures of the wild woods; he was a living cosmology! He also had the gift not of foresight but of future-sight. There is an enormous difference between the two. We use foresight when we look into the future and anticipate what we might encounter up ahead. Future-sight, however, is the result of being already in the future. It treats the future as familiar and known ground, as though it is already happening about you. . . .[2]

Like trends-mapping, scenario-building is at the heart of most futures-thinking methodologies. As images of a range of possible futures, the use of scenarios can provide a neutral space for collective discussion. By using stories to describe strategic issues, scenarios are more inclusive than many conventional conversational models, and represent a safe space in which differences of view can be uncovered and interrogated.

The success of a futures-thinking exercise also rests on the sequence through which trends and scenarios are explored. One such sequence is to move from consideration of a set of possibilities, to agreement on a set of more probable scenarios, to a consensus around a preferable future.

Making a conceptual distinction between possible, probable and preferred futures helps to uncover the very real tensions that accompany the business of making choices and to provide milestones in the journey taken by leaders thinking about the future. These are the design principles for any futures-thinking process.

Possible futures

There are any number of *possible* futures that could emerge, yet most people consider few that lie very far from their present reality. Often, individuals will slip automatically into talking about what they believe is likely, usually with a fatalistic tone. Encouraging a fuller investigation of possible futures forces people to reject the idea that 'what is' must be as it is and is all that can be or could be.

Probable futures

Opening things up tends to alter our perceptions of what is likely, so it is important that step one has been completed before moving on to step two: to identify what is probable. While avoiding fatalism, there are a number of factors, often concerning demographics, technology and global climate change over which we have little or no control, but which we must understand and deal with successfully. The most robust futures thinking takes account of 'known knowns' and also 'known unknowns'.

Preferred futures

These are the futures that people feel *should* come about. This is where values enter the process and provide a moral compass for assessing the desirability of different probable futures. Images of preferred futures are crucial because they provide hope and motivation for change. However, having explored the possible and probable, the goals and values which leaders started out with may have changed, or may, at the very least, require re-examination. Preferred futures can be constructed by breaking down different scenarios and reconstructing them in new ways.

Individuals can become futures literate by experiencing group processes and techniques designed to empower them in taking decisions for tomorrow today. In this sense, futures literacy centres on a strong belief in human agency. While all of us are embedded in organisations and cultures, we *can* act to change those organisations and cultures for the better if we so choose. But we need to find the tools and experiences which will build in us the confidence we need to take the plunge.

Matthew Horne and Helen McCarthy are researchers at Demos. This summary is adapted from a paper for the National College for School Leadership. Demos facilitated the two Scotland 2020 scenarios workshops, which were held in Edinburgh on 28 January and 24 March 2004. We would like to thank all the participants and the Scottish Book Trust for hosting the events.

Notes

1   The National College of School Leadership has been developing FutureSight as a tool for headteachers to use when thinking about the future of schooling. Demos has been working on FutureSight alongside the Department for Education and Skills and the OECD.

2   H Beare, *Creating the Future School* (London: Routledge Falmer, 2001), p 192.

4. Facing the New Atlantic

A short story by Ken MacLeod

As Scotland braces for its second winter without the Gulf Stream, we can be thankful that the emergency finds us well prepared. Wrapped and ready for the chill. Ten years ago, the outlook was nothing like so cosy. In 2010 the trends for health, population and employment pointed as relentlessly down as taxes, welfare dependency and summer temperatures trended up. Politicians sweated in the Holyrood glasshouse and squabbled over who was to pay for air conditioning. Investment and graduates headed south.

In the past ten years the country has changed.

You have to write about it, so you go to the pub, order a pot of coffee, set your frame on your nose and take a look around.

From the old lighthouse at Ness on the Butt of Lewis, you can see the icebergs. White against the grey, choppy water, they drift south, or erratically in other directions – the ocean currents, now that the Atlantic Conveyor and the Gulf Stream have shut down, are in a confused contraflow.

Like everything else.

You swing the view to the left and the south and look along the coast. Hundreds of wind-power generators stand along it, the long line of them extending past Borve and Shader to Carloway. The great blades turn, flashing where the sun catches them, as though signalling in some secret code to the iceberg fleet. Behind the straggled line of the windfarm, fat, super-conducting cables snake across machair and moorland, carrying power to the people. A sonic boom startles gannets and fulmars; the no-fly zone is low today, lower than the cloud cover, and the nominally joint patrols – European, Russian, American – jostle and joist above the sea to the northwest.

Cut across the Minch. You're not on the blacklist, so you can access a security camera overlooking a playground in Lochaber, under the blue-white slope of Ben Nevis. Kids yell and run, hurl snowballs. Snug in colourful, quilted gear from Mongolia or Koryo. Some of the faces are from these places, too. Pinned to every child's jacket is the regulation white plastic rectangle. You catch the habitual glances, the drilled-in check each child gives the other as they dash past, that the radiation badge hasn't turned black. Where you are, it's warm, but you shiver. (Like all of us, you remember where you were when . . .)

You ping the classroom. The jannie program scans your record and clears you in. The teacher nods in your direction, but that's just because she's noticed an indicator wink; you're part of a ghostly crowd of visitors – parents looking in, inspectors checking at random, passing journos, the idly curious – in one real and virtual corner of the room. There are twenty kids – sorry, students – in the real classroom, ten times that many in the virtual. Through windows you glimpse street scenes that suggest Kabul, Seoul, Harare, Caracas, Shanghai . . . you don't know. Wherever they are, the kids have frames under their eyes and bands on their wrists. The eyes dart, narrow in concentration; the fingers flex in the air, playing on invisible keyboards. The silence is a little eerie, but the teacher talks quietly here and there, to this child or that, and looks happier, less careworn, than you remember your own teachers ever having been.

It happens to be a non-smoking pub you're sitting in, doing this survey of the land, but your eyes sting a little. Too much time in the virtual. You reach up and lift your frame off, turn it over in your hands as the sounds and sights of the bar come back with a rush.

It's such a little thing, your frame, a scribbled line from some skeletal sketch of spectacles. A thin four-inch rod with a glassy bead on each end and a kink in the middle where it grips the bridge of your nose. As you turn it it glitters, as if set with tiny gems, as indeed it is:

the diamond lenses of the projectors that cast the images on your retina. The beads at the ends are cameras, and it's a trick that amuses children to patch the feed from them to your own eyes and suddenly see the scene in front of you in greater depth. Your wrist bands are likewise thin; you wear one of them under your watch, the other around your right wrist like an elastic band. They pick up your finger movements from the tendons. You slip the bands off and lay them on your palm with the frame: three tiny objects. No, five: you remember the equally unobtrusive pieces curled lightly around the backs of your ears, and take them off too. Five, then: a set. Stamped out by the billion, in factory processes pioneered in Scotland's own 'Carbon Glen', they've changed the world. Or so the hype goes. The mobile phone and the personal computer did no less in their day. Or so the debunking goes.

It's hard to say whether the debunkers or the boosters are right. Certainly, the early hope that seamless, comfortable virtual environments and workspaces would make routine commuting and business travel unnecessary haven't been borne out. Terrorism, recessions, environmental taxes and viral epidemics have hammered international air travel. But local air travel has increased: the busy triangular air shuttle between Edinburgh, Glasgow and Inverness has counterparts across Europe. Global travellers take the ekranoplans, the ships that fly a couple of metres above the waves, and that can cross the Atlantic in fourteen hours. The Clydeside yards are busy again.

The afternoon light is waning. The coffee's long gone cold. You're considering ordering a refill when half a dozen guys in orange waterproof, windproof Highway overalls come in, swaggering, off-shift, talking loud, laughing, calling for pints. Laggers. It used to be a respectable sneer-word, like 'ned' or 'numpty' or 'schemie', and applied to much the same kind of people – those left out of the information economy, those who lagged behind. These days it's what they call themselves, and proudly. If you can't hack programs, design or stamp out frames, teach students, distil whisky, grow hemp or build ekranoplans, you can lag pipes. (You have to. It's hi-tech or the

Highway. As a First Minister once said: 'Insulation, insulation, insulation.' It was an exasperated moment, a hot afternoon, a hotter debate, but the opposition parties and the *Record* didn't let her live it down. She was right, though that's cold comfort for her. She now designs healthcare packages in Pretoria.) You can lay super-conducting cables. You can build the new underground houses in the Barratt Homes hobbitt-towns. The energy-saving work of the laggers has – quite unexpectedly, quite unplanned – fortuitously and fortunately prepared us for the big chill. But even they aren't enough, and more is needed. We're pulling in diaspora exiles who know how to cope with it better than we do: Newfoundlanders and Nova Scotians (doubling the number of Gaelic speakers, funnily enough) and obscure Siberian descendants of forgotten Czarist-era Scottish engineers. Vodka on Burns Night! Is nothing sacred? Wrong question. We need all the change we can get to make the changes we need.

There are other, less welcome immigrants. Less welcome, because less welcoming. People who in the past decade or so have taken 'Western Europe's last great wilderness' as something more than a Tourist Board slogan, who think it's the last White North. Odd little clots of malcontents from Southern France or Eastern Europe, setting up as survivalists in the wet deserts of the Western Highlands. They cook their food and clothes with strange experimental molecular machines, huddle in polymer teepees, poach deer and (the rumour goes) steal cattle. How they'll cope with the coming big freeze isn't hard to predict: another rumour runs that all the Highway work teams in the Highlands have someone riding shotgun, these days, but you've never seen the evidence.

But that's not the note to end on. The separatist survivalists are a minor nuisance. Scotland has faced down bigger problems. There are bigger ones to come, in a world where the south is heating up and the north is cooling down, where every current is in contraflow, where much that was solid melts and much that once seemed vapour is freezing and condensing out of the air. Where the air is clear of smoke, but sparkles with unseen menace from the dirty bombs and the counterstrikes.

You put away your frames, wave your wrist over the table's billpoint, sidle past the laughing laggers and out into the street. As you step through the door you glance down at the plastic rectangle pinned to your lapel. It stays clear. You breathe in and walk out. Past new flags and old, past a snow-covered statue of a gaunt man with glasses – it could be Donald Dewar, it could be Edwin Morgan – through the street where the changes began and continue, and you take the train a hundred kilometres home in twenty minutes, and you think about Scotland and your article and you wonder what you're going to write.

5. The Imagineers

A short story by Julie Bertagna

A sky the colour of tarpaulin hangs over the land. Arctic smite threshes the windfarms of the Atlantic Energy Isles, soon to hit the mainland. Stand at the river by the old dockyard crane. Listen. The wind that travels the ice path of the Clyde carries the death bellow of bergs, collapsing, beyond the Firth and the Sounds, making ice soup of the Atlantic and the Irish Sea. The noise of a world's end. At night, when the nation's lights go out, even the sparking web of the trams, the glimmer and groan of the bergs spook a deep, starless dark.

He'll stop at the next café, for coffee and a read. Walking gets him out of an empty house, fends off the cold, saves on heating rations too. Though it's almost summer, as his generation stubbornly call it, the berg bite penetrates the defences of double glazing, thermal curtains, wall insulation and head to toe polar synthetics. He's pocketed Morgan's *Cathures* for his walk along the Clyde, bought second-hand, as most books are now paper is as rationed as heat. The book crackles at his touch, tinder in the pages.

When winter became the only season, we came to know the temper of a new Dark Age. We dug into language, found as many names as the weather had moods. Now, there was never just cold, wind, rain, snow. There was welt, froar, smite, whelm, thresh. Sometimes it was withershin, or a sleetmidden of a day. The act of naming was primeval, an urge to tame forces beyond control.

A rivercutter churns a path through the ice. Will negotiates his own path through the iceboarders who weave between the trunks of the wind turbines that line the banks of the Clyde. There's a grace in the sweep of the blades that's almost, Will has come to think, as majestic as an avenue of oaks. He passes the church with the broken spire, and the site of the red sandstone school where he was headteacher, once. Now gone, in its place is the *McConndillo*, as it's known, the McConnell Research Institute, the largest of the armadillos that breed beside the river. There's an almighty clatter as the threatened Arctic smite, hard as gravel, hits the armadillo shells.

The education system reached breaking point by 2010: teacher exodus, sink schools empty, popular ones chock full, a chaos of choice, rocketing truancy, exam system fiasco, classroom violence, deepening cuts in education as the ageing population gobbled public sector funds. Independent schools boomed; some bust, as a crop of cheaper, industry-funded ones made private education less elite. A movement for home schools gathered pace, resourced on a shoestring by Library Discovery Zones, the internet, electronic books. Suddenly, education was up for grabs.

The virus was the last straw. It came with the muggy monsoon of 2012, the end of a run of tropical summers that had us fooled into dreams of Perthshire Pinot and Clyde Valley Chardonnay, sipped beside the garden pool. The media, in full apocalyptic mode, blamed the epidemic on migrant workers, asylum seekers. The numbers of deaths weren't high, fear more infectious than the virus itself. Now, even pupils who had stayed to the last, abandoned school.

Will hurries to the nearest armadillo for shelter from the smite. A waft of coffee draws him inside, where he finds a mass of young people huddled around tables. The focused energy is palpable. He sees a lad take a tube of blue plastic from his pocket, he unrolls it into a keyboard, clips on a small transmitter chip like an earring. They've all got them. *Godboxes.* A technological wizardry that's beyond Will. The stuff of science fiction a decade ago, the *godbox* is to this generation what the mobile phone and laptop were to his.

An astonishing vision covers the armadillo's arched ceiling. Its theme is Alasdair Gray's inspiration to *work as if you live in the early days of a better nation.* Whether it's authentic Gray or the work of his Michelangelo-style apprentices, it's impossible to tell. Will gazes, entranced.

Even before the breakdown, the young sussed that the old education was defunct. Galloping technology had given them a radical, widescreen vision of the world. Globalists, they also knew the crumbling infrastructure of their immediate world, where there was a new black market in plumbing, bricklaying, damp-proofing, nursing. At the start of the new school year in August 2012, Will Moss, like headteachers across the land, stood in the empty corridor of a ghost school and admitted defeat.

In the doorway of the armadillo, Linda shakes off a melting crust of smite. She has to manoeuvre the buggy past an elderly man who's staring open-mouthed at the ceiling. When he pulls down the hood of his weathergear, she sees it's Mr Moss. At school she was such a wee minx, a real stirrer, flung out of class time and again for being mouthy. Acting like you had all the answers was how you survived at Brae High. She parks the buggy beside a table, checks Sam under his weathershield, but he's well zonked after a night's teething and a morning's finger-painting. The dummy drops from his sleep-heavy mouth. They often come back to the hub after she collects him from morning nursery. Sam naps and plays with the toy boxes. She has an extra coffee, chats, does a bit more work. Mr Moss looks lost. Linda knows the feeling. She felt it most days at Brae High.

Weather saved the kids when the schools packed up. They couldn't hang about the streets, getting up to no good. The weather was too bad. Crime, alcohol and drugs didn't obliterate a generation as the prophets of doom predicted – at least, no more than before. Freed from the mass policing and hoop-jumping of the classroom while politicians, parents, educationists and the media fought across the ruins of the education system, the young stole away. They huddled in bedrooms and cafés, engrossed in themselves and each other, and in the wonders of the new technology, their doorway to the world.

Will takes a seat beside the young woman, awkward and smiling, who's waved him over. One of his ex-pupils, Linda Mullen, of all people. The last girl he'd expect to be sitting here telling him she was an apprentice imagineer in this brave new world of godboxes and Arctic whelm. An imagineer, she says, is an engineer of ideas. Bet *you* never imagined a waster like me would ever get to be that, eh, Mr Moss? Oh, you always had ideas, Linda, he retorts, just the wrong ones in the wrong place at the wrong time. She laughs, tells him now she's in the right place and it's her old talent for being mouthy that helped her get a foot in the door as a connector, communicating with imagineers all over the world. That and getting pregnant.

After the schools shut she had a gap year of sorts, tripping with a lost boy, like so many Will has known – old men at ten, emotional brick walls, wasted or dead before they were twenty. She meant to get rid of the baby but the health centre treated her like royalty, sat her down and told her about *New Life* – benefits, childcare, access to education, tax benefits when you started work, and a mother-buddy scheme. If she wanted the baby she'd be given the necessary help. The birth rate crisis had made heroes of young mothers. For the first time in her life Linda felt important.

Wendy Knox metamorphosed from young nursery teacher into political activist in the nursery workers' pay dispute of 2004. A decade later, as a Junior Minister for Education, she led an investigation into why eager pre-schoolers were truants by age twelve. When the education system imploded, pulling down the First Minister and much of the Education team with it, Wendy Knox was found alone among the rubble at ground zero, clutching her report, 'Enterprising Education – The Way Forward'. Inspired by the active learning which nursery children thrived on, 'The Way Forward' was almost lost under a weight of expectation and ridicule. It was the tabloids, who decided to champion the photogenic MSP Knox, that saved Wendy's Way.

If she hadn't had Sam, Linda reckons she wouldn't be here now. The turning point was gaining a set of keys that opened up the future. She yawns, takes a gulp of coffee. Will is beginning to understand. They're trying to turn negatives into positives, these young imagineers. They're imagineering the world, the weather, connecting global ideas on all kinds of things – flood-protection, all-weather railways, deep-sea wavepower, offshore windfarming, water exports to combat drought; even *Coolbreaks Scotland*, holiday relief from the soaring temperatures of global warming in other parts of the world. *As predicted, the population aged and the birth rate plummeted. What wasn't predicted was intergenerational war. Political parties fragmented. Policies for the Young were at odds with the needs of the Old. At thirty-six, the Internationalist First Minister Knox was just mature enough to be taken seriously by the Old and just youthful enough to be accepted by the Young. She brought the warring generations together over education, persuading older people they were essential to its success. Small group learning proved more effective than any recruitment drive. A massive public advertising campaign was launched to promote the inquisitive play ethic of the New Way. A drift back to school began.*

There was a time of confusion. But the onslaught of Arctic weather saw the rebirth of the local school. And infecting education with the virus of enterprise was, it turned out, the most powerful form of mass vaccination against the malady that had afflicted generations of Scots (except the diaspora of those with freak immunity). Lack of confidence. Nicknamed Steemies, the new schools' core curriculum was self-esteem. A flexible leaving age led into apprenticeships, further education or indie-enterprise. A stagnant backwater in the modern economy, Scotland began to re-envision itself as fertile land for the cultivation of ideas. As a land of imagineers.

There's a nudge at Will's foot. The little boy, Sam, is out of his buggy and under the table, playing with bricks. He's struggling to build a bridge. Will can see what's wrong. He's about to tell the child when Sam tears thumb from mouth, knocks down the old bridge, scattering bricks all across the floor.

As the climate bitters, there's a move inland. Terrorism and gridlock bring a wave of English migrants north to the green metropolis of multicultural glentowns. Perth is the gateway, a city of commerce for the weatherworkers of the Highland windfarms and the new industries. The brain drain, reversed, is brain flame.

There is no happy ever after. Weather is our war. There's still homelessness, crime, rubbish and drugs on the streets, racism against 'migs' and 'seeks'. Pensions are still a shambles, health a national disgrace. The timbers of the public sector creak and crack. And still the glasses on Donald Dewar's statue need fixing. But the energy and imagination of the young, globalist, free from the harness of another age, is active.

Will hunkers down under the table and picks up one of the old, wooden bricks. He hears the heavy breathing of a child's deep concentration. Sam gives him a wet smile from behind the thumb that's stuck back in his mouth. Will sticks his own thumb in his mouth and smiles a mirror greeting that makes Sam laugh. The industry of the coffee machine and the workers at the tables makes a cocoon of noise that muffles the weather battering the armadillo. At the feet of the imagineers, Will and the child huddle together and start to build.

6. Scotland the Grave

A short story by Pennie Taylor

Scotland's history is a long tale of fortitude in the face of adversity. Barring a few brief bursts of optimism – Bannockburn, the Enlightenment, the reformation of the Scottish Parliament – it is a catalogue of near-miss and failure. Over time, Scots have evolved an innate fatalism, yet they still cling to the collective dream that one day they will grasp power again.

Sentimental notions of the nation characterise the world view too. Faced with plummeting visitor numbers because of the ongoing Terrorist Wars, the tourism authorities have abandoned all hope of promoting a forward-looking and funky Scotland. Instead, they have resorted to blackmail-by-billboard and mercilessly tug at the heartstrings of the Scottish diaspora with images of 'claymore culture'.

Attracted by generous public subsidy, a multinational entertainment conglomerate has built a vast interactive theme park at Harthill. Here, visitors are invited to experience the romantic highlights of Scotland's past – step into the virtual shoes of a refugee from Glencoe, ride with Robert the Bruce, or march with Bonnie Prince Charlie's army, perhaps.

The venture has been a qualified success. School parties use it to illustrate the history syllabus and ticket sales have been on target, but overseas visitors are far outnumbered by young Scots who come from all over the country to wage war on computerised battlefields. The revival of old enmities has overtaken football as the national passion, and the resulting riots have attracted worldwide media attention. 'Clash of the Clans' is now broadcast live each week on Japanese TV.

Making it in the media – one way or another – is a popular ambition among Scotland's disenfranchised young. More than half still leave school at 16, and television projects a world far removed from their reality.

Between 2004 and 2020 the population of Scotland sank to an all-time low. One-child families are now the norm, and increasing numbers of women are rejecting motherhood altogether. Despite the best efforts to persuade qualified Scots to stay in the country, there is net migration of people of working age, and decades of successful interventional healthcare mean that there are more people aged 70 and over than ever before. Despite marginal tax rises, the burden on the public purse is increasingly heavy – and some say unsustainable.

Within a Scottish Parliament made up of rump parties and a wide range of independents, discussion rages about how to tackle the problems but as no consensus is ever reached, change never happens. Westminster subsidy is under constant threat, and the media revels in predicting imminent disaster. The public, however, is not willing to engage in the debate about solutions. Most want things to stay just as they are – come what may.

Driven by a passion to protect the founding principles of the National Health Service, Scotland has maintained – and even extended – free care for all. As a result, older people and the chronically ill from south of the border (and across Europe) have taken up residence in the communities that are expanding around the country's five major acute hospitals.

Healthcare is something of a national industry. It is the country's largest employer by far and high concentrations of disease, especially in the West of Scotland, have attracted clusters of scientists and researchers who are now leading the world in developing effective treatments for previously incurable diseases.

Bioscience companies are flourishing in Glasgow, Edinburgh and Dundee and the revenue they generate has buoyed the economy, but there is the constant threat of losing the edge to the Far East and Asia where the bio- and nanotechnology sectors are expanding fast.

Financial incentives for those who take science subjects at Scottish universities have significantly boosted student numbers, and there is a home-grown pool of talent for the industry to draw upon – although that is a fragile resource. Scottish universities, which are not permitted to raise fees independently, have to fight long and hard for the public funding they need to retain the world-ranking academics and maintain their status.

As there are no tuition charges in Scotland there is a cross-border influx of undergraduates, which imposes severe pressure on capacity. But, despite high-level attempts to persuade them to stay on, most postgraduates tend to leave the country as soon as they can.

Prospects for employment are limited. Glasgow is the focus for creative industries and enjoys a worldwide reputation for high-end bespoke technocraft products, but the most successful companies are small and do not generate jobs. Edinburgh remains the country's most prosperous city, and it is the only urban population to continue to expand, but the capital's wealth is not shared.

The social inclusion initiatives of the past two decades appear to have done little to influence the gap between rich and poor. At one end of the spectrum are the entrepreneurs who have grasped globalisation and turned it to their advantage, and the innovators who have made fortunes from drug and health technology developments that are selling around the world. At the other extreme are the millions with no pensions who are dependent on an increasingly over-stretched state. As well as a disproportionate number of the old there are the chronically ill: diseases such as diabetes and asthma are rife in all age groups, and obesity among children is approaching 40%.

There is a burgeoning middle class, largely made up of those who have inherited wealth from parents or built it up during the 2006 Scottish property boom. And because public sector pensions have been protected, there are cohorts of retired healthworkers, teachers and other professionals who expect an adequate income into old age.

These so-called 'silver spenders' are a lucrative market, and intensively targeted by advertisers. Instead of saving for old age, there is a trend towards releasing equity and liquidating assets. After all, in Scotland all care for the elderly is free.

Taxpayers are concerned about the sustainability of the economy and several attempts have been made to have expensive policies re-examined; however, debate never gets far. The print media, slugging it out for survival in a shrinking market, threaten to incite revolution every time welfare reforms are suggested. Instead, the sports and culture budget is cut again: there is now one national arts company for Scotland, incorporating the former national orchestra, ballet and opera company, and the few remaining football clubs are going bust. Despite sustained state support the Gaelic language is dying out, and continuing subsidy cannot be justified for long.

Defenders of the status quo cite the positive effects on the national psyche brought about by the caring Scotland: it is a more tolerant society, where economic immigrants from all over the world are welcomed for the contribution they can make, and there has been a reduction in the stigma associated with age, gender issues and mental health. Per capita, Scots may still be Europe's highest users of antidepressants – but at least they are talking about it now!

The gender profile of the workforce continues to shift. There are now more women in full-time employment than men, and female students make up the majority at university level. The traditionally male industries are gone, and there has been a particularly harsh impact on remote and rural communities: the last fishing boat in Scotland was scuppered five years ago, and intensive agriculture shuddered to a halt with the global chicken flu epidemic, and the concurrent resurgence of foot-and-mouth disease and a series of pesticide scares.

Devastating terrorist attacks on airlines and exorbitant travel insurance have led to the development of extremely sophisticated global communications, and home-working is commonplace, particularly in the IT and financial sectors. There are concerns about isolation, which has been linked to an increase in female alcohol problems and persistently high suicide rates among Scottish males, many more of whom now live alone.

The world oil shortage caused by depleted resources and political chaos in the Middle East has priced imports out of the market, and there has been a growth in Scottish manufacturing. Environmentalists are concerned about rising CO_2 emissions and ozone depletion (the incidence of skin cancers has been increasing steadily, and large areas of the country are now uninhabitable because of flooding), but there will be no new policies to limit pollution because of a potentially adverse effect on trade.

Snow in Scotland is a thing of the past, and the skiing industry finally bit the dust in 2008. It may be markedly warmer these days, but it also rains a great deal more and mosquitoes have joined the midgie swarms that make so much of the country impassable during the summer months. Overseas visitors typically make the trip to the 'auld country' only once, and tourism is struggling to survive.

While many Scots feel victimised by the knock-on effects of global epidemics, politics and the impact of environmental pollution, there are a few visionaries who are keen to capitalise on the potential these world forces also represent.

Self-sufficiency is now an imperative. Because of the necessity for more food to be produced domestically, small-scale farming is undergoing a revival, with organic growers in particular experiencing a boom. The nation's diet is starting to improve, as Scots denied easy access to mass-produced burgers and chips turn to healthy home-grown produce and re-learn long-lost cooking skills.

However, it is the implosion of the oil markets of the Middle East that holds the greatest promise for the Scots' economy. There is now worldwide demand for alternative sources of energy, and Scotland has all the raw ingredients – in spades. Hydroelectricity, wind and wave power generation could put the country at the top of the economic leagues, and establish it as a world force. Real power, in a modern sense, is finally within the nation's grasp.

7. Intervention

A short story by Ruaridh Nicoll

Lydia lifted her creepers onto the desk and tightened the laces without looking. Her gaze was on the horizon, the city shearing in towards her feet. There was a whisper of a breeze from the west, Spring easing its way through the narrow gap in the window, the air fresh at the top of the new government building in Drumchapel. She had a habit of checking her shoes before she went out; country-bred, she disliked crouching too close to the street. Her diary was by her foot, and she searched for the address. It was April, and she couldn't believe she had turned twenty.

Andy Wightman was leaning against the wall, reading the sports pages of the *Record*. He was eating a bacon and egg roll from Hassan's, the greasy spoon that had set up outside the office on the day the building opened, so now the yellow cards advertising eggs, beans and chips hung only yards from the steel plaque announcing 'Health Scotland!' A drool of yolk fell from the bun onto the newspaper, yellowing the cheek of the national football coach. 'That about sums that up,' said Lydia. Scotland had fallen in a friendly to Norway.

'Say merde,' said Andy (Didier Agathe, the coach, was French). 'So where's Miss Motivator off to today?'

'Down river.'

'A hefty?'

'Maybe. Hasn't worked in sixteen years so a lost soul, whoever he is.' Lydia disliked Andy's weariness with their job, his lack of conviction that it was possible to convince people they were actually healthy. She still did her homework, spending her evenings reading the files and trying to imagine the person caught under the stamp marked 'DISABLED', looking for the character in the ailments listed in the benefit claims and the patchy notes of other civil servants. She decided against telling him of the lost hopes she had seen in the notes for David Liddell. 'What about you?'

'Stuck here. I was supposed to be talking up fruit and veg for the staff of. . .' He paused and leaned forward, reading from a pad that lay on his desk. '. . .Woodline Paper, but then I phoned to confirm and a recorded voice said they had gone bust.'

'Well, given that bun, they probably got off lightly.'

'Come to terms with your hypocrisy, Lydia, and a happy life awaits you.'

* * *

Roadworks on the Kingston bridge had caused a tailback, and Lydia sat smiling at the vast plasma-banner the city councillors had recently slung across the blue trusses of the gas tanks. It had been the retiring wish of Sir Peter Irvine, chairman of Culture Scotland, that Glasgow drop its slogan, and instead go with 'Glasgow's a Gas', above constantly changing, often disconcerting, portraits of the city's inhabitants taken by a camera in George Square. Her attention was caught by a child gurning at her from the back of one of those ubiquitous hybrid cars that looked like urinating frogs. Lydia made a face back but the exchange drew out and soon she felt uncomfortable with the intimacy. She willed the traffic to move until it did, and she found she could see the mountains.

She felt hungry, and thought of the seafood she would eat in the garden in Lochcarron. Her parents – 'spoilers', as the *West Highland Free Press* had taken to calling the retiring baby-boom generation – had chosen the slim Wester Ross town as an affordable alternative to Skye when they left Chester. Lydia thought they had been lucky in the choice; Lochcarron still had its young, particularly Hugh Anderson, a game manager on the community estate. As she thought of him, of that so un-gym physique she had yet to touch, she began pressing her toes against the inside of her shoes. She reached out to where her Smartphone was lodged in the dash, pressing the button that allowed her to dictate a quick text: 'In traffic jam, how're the hills?'

The cars shifted again, and the child was beside once more, face to the glass, bringing her back. All that money spent on advertising, she thought with a sudden distaste, and nothing changes, the few kids women felt inclined to produce turned out to be wee bladders. She tried to forget her text and focus on the man she was due to see, and the difficulty of lecturing a man who had been off work almost as long as she had been alive. The Smartfone rang, simultaneously quietening the ElectroClash it had been playing. Lydia pressed 'accept' and heard a slow whup-whup-whup emerge from the speaker. 'Unbelievable,' she said. 'You really are on the mountain.'

He laughed. 'You can hear the turbine. I've got my tea. I'm looking out west. Spring's in the air. The islands are black in a shimmering sea. Where are you not managing to get to?'

'Greenock.'

'Who's the lucky victim?'

'David Liddell.' She pressed the screen of her diary. 'Post viral exhaustion, depression, bad back, and all due to some long-ago injury to his left hand.' There was a blast from the car behind, the traffic was moving again. Lydia accelerated as she imagined Hugh sitting there, leaning forward slightly, smiling sympathetically as he listened. 'So you can see why I am thinking of trying out the fast new train this weekend.'

'You should. We're playing Kingussie at home.'

The thought of him on the shinty pitch pleased her. 'So I'll have to hang out on the sidelines with your fan club?' She had recently grown fond of spectator sports. She liked the calm assertiveness he had, violence erupting only if there were relatives on the other team.

'Aye right. You would be my entire fan club.'

The last time she had watched him play, she had been with Jean Urquhart. They had spent the entire match giggling over his thighs and calves. She decided to hold that thought. 'We're just about to go

through the underpass. I'll call you when I arrive.'
'You do that. Now go and wake the dead.'

* * *

Lydia pulled up halfway along Haulderon Road, and stepped out of the Nokiaka. The houses, part of the Clydeside regeneration, were already past their best, their waterside setting let down by lousy construction. A few of the properties had been looked after and she found herself guiltily suspecting that those were inhabited by immigrants. The sun was warm, calming the nervousness she always felt before first contact. Liddell's house had one of the SNP's 'Bring Back the Barnett' stickers in the window, the so-mocked picture of convener Andrew Wilson's ageing bouffant beside it.

Liddell took a moment to open the door and, when he did, he looked her up and down. 'You this Lydia?' He was a big man, but not obese, and, unusually, he looked ill. The remnants of a wasted strength hung on his body. 'The government likes its humiliations, doesn't it? Ah'm tae be told to get on ma bike by a teenager.'

'I'm not here to tell you to do anything.'

There was something beaten about him as he stepped back. 'Well, come in then,' he said. 'I canny bear the sun.' For this, the house suited him; the hall existed in darkness and the kitchen in gloom, a stain of sunlight spreading through the net curtains. The kitchen was clean, a rare blessing for Lydia, and he pointed her to a stool at the table, groaning himself into a garden chair. 'So you're here to take ma benefits, then?' As he spoke he dropped his left hand on the table; it extended to only two fingers and half a thumb.

'That's not my job.'

A girl, only a couple of years younger than Lydia, had wandered into the room. Her eyes were set wide, and there was an elegance to her that sat oddly with her age and background. 'Well, if that's the case, have a cup of tea,' she said.

'Faith, my too generous daughter,' said Liddell. 'The wife's at work.' His chair sat opposite a screen. The girl switched it on, but only so that she could record a programme on the cookery channel before she turned it off again.

'My job is to see if we can get you contributing again.' Lydia took in the room as she spoke, her gaze coming to rest on a postcard of the Parliament pinned above the old-fashioned stove. She must have paused. Liddell did not need to look to see what had caught her attention.

'That's where it happened,' he said. 'One of Miralles' bloody leaf windas didnie fit and fell on ma hand.'

'And the rest? The back, the post-viral exhaustion?'

Faith had put the mug down, along with a plate of oatcakes and jam.

'What are you givin her her tea for?' Liddell was outraged, but his tone was one of speaking to an equal, the faint sense of threat was for Lydia alone.

'Oh hush,' said Faith.

There was a silence. Lydia asked again about the exhaustion.

'Ma back, I did fightin with some bastard outside a pub, over the bloody Parliament no less. He said it was shite and I belted him, wi this, and . . .' – he lifted the hand – 'it got infected, and I never recovered from that. I'm fucked, not to put too fine a point on it, so eat yer cakes and take yer psychology elsewhere.'

Lydia picked up one of the oatcakes and bit down on it. The taste actually shocked her and she coughed. 'Faith, these are beautiful. They're home-made?'

'Not just the cakes, the jam too,' Faith answered.

'They're the best I've ever tasted.'

'Aye well, you're young yet,' said Liddell. He reached over and took one with his ruined hand. 'So who's the next poor sap ye reckon needs to make a contribution?'

'Please, Mr Liddell, let me say my piece. I'm here because we, the government and other civil servants like me, have convinced too many people they are ill when they're not. At the moment, according to Work and Pensions, twenty-eight percent – *nearly one in three* – of the workforce are on disability in this area.'

'And you reckon most of them are skivin?'

'No. Very few are. Most believe they are ill because the government has spent years telling them they are, just to get them off the unemployed register. Tell people that for long enough and they will believe it. People are ill because they've been told they are.'

'Not me.' He showed his hand.

'I'm not belittling it, Mr Liddell, but it's one hand. Is there nothing you want to do? Don't you have any hobbies?'

He laughed. 'I like the telly and I like sleeping with my wife. Can I make a new career out o' that?'

Faith's head turned away, as if she were looking through the curtains, and Lydia sighed.

'Doesn't it get depressing? Staying inside, feeling ill. I know I'm young, but here we are, we've all got something to offer . . . look at Faith, with that cooking, those oatcakes, that jam.'

'What makes you think they are mine?' Faith said.

'Faith!' barked Liddell.

Lydia said nothing for a moment, and then she smiled. She looked from one to the other. This was going to be a good day. The future was hers to lose now, but she would handle David Liddell carefully. It would be several weeks before she would mention the farmers' hypermarket in this house. It was enough to have found a reason, and an ally. At that moment, she decided that Hugh would be hers that weekend. She would offer to rub salve on his post-match wounds, and she would take him iodine as a present. She would touch those thighs. She took another bite of oatcake and looked from Liddell to his daughter, from anger to resolve, and knew, as long as she kept her head, she had won. For, in this house, she had love on her side.

8. The Tartan Initiative

A short story by Anne Donovan

Oh ye cannae shove yer granny aff a bus
Oh ye cannae shove yer granny aff a bus
Oh ye cannae shove yer granny
Fur she's yer mammy's mammy
Ye cannae shove yer granny aff a bus.

Well, that's whit ah'm singin anyroad. The weans are singin, 'You cannae shove your granny *off* a bus'. Ah tried tae tell them it was *aff*, no *off* but they don't get it.

I don't like saying aff – it doesn't sound right.

Doesnae.

Whatever . . . what difference does it make anyway?

Well, it has tae be aff – it's Scots.

I'm Scottish and I say off.

Anyway, it's assonance.

Duh?

Assonance – internal rhyme – granny, cannae, mammy, aff, all have an 'a' sound – if you say 'off' it doesnae sound as good.

Sir, the bell's gone.

The bell's went, you mean. Ah was only hauf-jokin.

Samira's eyes rolled heavenward.

OK, pack up, noo.

They stampeded oot. Ms Tierney emerged fae the back row,

snappin shut her laptop as she negotiated the row a desks.
Assonance, Jim . . . is that not a bit advanced?
For them or for a numpty like me, d'ye mean?
She smiled, then daundered alang tae the staffroom, leavin me tae
log aff the system.

* * *

The Scots language project forms a key strand in the Tartan Initiative
and combines several objectives of the Scottish Executive:

> *In order to comply with the EEC report on Minority Languages
> (Status 2) the Executive, while not necessarily promoting the
> Scots language, should not allow its further decline.*

> *There is a need to address the significant underemployment of
> males aged between 44 and 65.*

> *Given that the proportion of female teachers has now risen to
> 93% in the secondary sector, there is concern at the lack of male
> role models in educational establishments.*

* * *

Sounded brilliant when they tellt me aboot it at the Jobcentre – sorry
– Individual Enterprize Zone. Coupla sessions a week at a local school
just bletherin wi the weans, singin a few songs, playin games.
    *A teacher'll be present all the time – it's just so they can listen to a
Scots voice.*
    Scots – ah'm no wanny they hoochter choochers.
    Yes but you're a Scots speaker.
    Ah'm are?
    The wumman clicked on the form.
    *Key in yout pin number, Mr McKeown. These taster sessions will be
assessed to see if you are suitable to train as a classroom assistant, maybe
even a teacher eventually.*

But ah'm nearly sixty. Whit's the point in spendin money trainin me? Ah'll be retired in five year.

Policy change. Have you not received an email yet? They're raising the retiral age to 75. And with in-house modular learning you could be employed for the next fifteen years.

Ironic when you think of all the years ah spent in ma twenties, signin on every week, desperate for a job. Everythin had collapsed roond wer ears: minin, shipyerds. Us guys that left school at sixteen, lookin tae follow wer faithers intae a trade were scuppered by Thatcher, relyin oan the wife's wee job in the supermarket tae keep the hoose gaun. Then efter Maggie was oot, oot, oot for good, we got part time in B&Q, homers, computer trainin courses, but never a real job in all that time. Noo they want tae send us nickin roond classrooms on wer zimmers.

Still anythin's better than sittin lookin at four walls and ah'd get a tenner on tappy ma dole money – sorry Non-Enterprize Related Income. Sent me on an online trainin course. The teacher was this wee auld guy used tae be a uni professor in Scottish Mediaeval Literature. Tellt us we spoke urban Scots – we'd tae take it in turns tae tell the others sumpn that happened tae us.

You might have gone on a holiday, perhaps.

Aye right.

It felt daft, talkin intae a computer. The hardest bit was learnin that the words ah always thought were slang or just plain wrang, like 'ah've went' or 'ah done' are actually Scots grammatical forms. The wee Prof gied us a list of books and websites and ah read up oan it: lexical features, register, discourse, assonance. Goat all fired up aboot keepin the language alive, even though ah'd never realised it was a language afore.

Strange gaun intae a school again but. Hud tae get checked oot by the polis, then they sent me an ID card wi an iris imprint. And the first day ah'd tae get searched and go through a metal detector.

When ma weans were wee the parents watched them line up in the yard, waved at them as they followed the teacher inside. If they were late we took them intae their classroom. But when ma youngest grandson started school three year ago his mammy wasnae even allowed intae the playground on the first day. All the weans are checked in like parcels. You go through an outer door wi a metal detector, key in their date of birth and they enter the next lobby by theirsels and put in a pin number tae get let inside the school. The parents arenae even supposed tae know their wean's pin number. And the playgrounds are all surrounded by high walls so naebdy can see in. They built them aboot seven year ago – ma Kevin's a brickie and he got a loatty work that year.

That was aboot the same time they done away wi uniforms. No that many of the weans wore them anyway, least no roond here, but there was a big fuss aboot it. The politicians said they were tryin tae make us mair European. Issued the weans wi white labcoats tae cover their claes and started givin oot croissants at the Breakfast Club.

Noo there's the Tartan Initiative. Every wean has tae wear a tartan badge in the shape of a Scottie dug, printed wi their school name and 'Scotland's brand – Scotland's grand'.

* * *

Next day this other lassie came alang tae unlock the door.

Hi – I'm Gemma McIntyre.

She'd a big stud in her tongue. Early thirties, wearin a suit but loadsa ear-rings and a wee sparkly stud in her nose. Didnae think they let teachers go aboot like that, even nooadays.

She sat at the backy the class, got on wi her markin. The teachers have laptops and the weans dae their work on computers and email it tae them, so there's nae mair jotters wi red pens all ower them. Neat, tidy. Only thing is the weans cannae write any mair. Kevin's boy, Jack – he's seventeen and his writin looks like a six year auld's.

As the lesson, well if you could cry it a lesson, went on, Gemma lifted her heid fae her work as if she was listenin in. Ah was startin tae get a bit uncomfortable, wondered if ah was daein sumpn wrang even though we were only talkin aboot kids' games and that. And at the end, insteidy lockin up and heidin aff she said, *D'you want to come along for a cup of tea?*

The notice ootside said 'Staff Preparation and Recreation Area'. Ah mind when ah was wee catchin a glimpse of a staffroom fae an open door: a guddle of books and papers, manky auld mugs and a noticeboard wi a few ancient cuttins, turnin yella. This base was immaculate; dookets at wan end wi rechargers for the laptops, a watter fountain and tea and coffee vendin machine wi a big sign: 'Two a day only – cut down caffeine for health and productivity'.

You need to put in your pin number.

Havenae got wan. Ah'm no counted as staff.

I'll do without – oh wait a minute, Nazia's off – what's her number, Paula?

Anither young yin in a power suit and dreadlocks lifted her heid fae a screen.

3672 – I think Lulyeta had one already though.

Gemma keyed it in. *Tea or coffee?*

Coffee with mulk, two sugars – what is all this? D'yous no have a kettle and teabags?

Sugar – you're kidding – it'd be easier to get cocaine. They introduced these machines about four years ago – said it was unsafe to have our own kettles. Then last year when the second Caffeine Report came out they restricted everyone to two cups a day – for health reasons, they said.

Miserable bastards don't want to pay for it, said Paula.

I'd be happy to pay for it myself, said Gemma. *I just drink twice as much at home.*

She haunded me the cup.

So how are you enjoying the Scots module?

Dunno – it's OK. Ah thought the weans would really like it, but – when ah was at school ah'd of been dead chuffed if somebody came in and talked in ma ain language but they don't seem bothered.

It's not their language any more though.

Surely some of them must talk like that at hame.

Don't think so.

Ah sat for a minute, drinkin the tea. It tasted as if it'd been made wi watter that's no boiled.

Listen, d'you fancy coming in to help me with a project?

Ah'm no a teacher.

That's the point. My third year are doing a language topic and it's dead boring. Language and Identity Module.

Paula snorted.

I've got an idea about doing something more in depth, more real. All you'd need to do is chat to them – I'd be taking the class.

OK.

Tomorrow at ten?

* * *

Ah was dead impressed when ah seen her in action. The weans nooadays are giants – some of the big laddies looked like men – ah thought they'd mibbe of been at it wi a wee lassie like her but they settled doon right away. She was that confident, fulla energy, jumpin aboot fae wan sidey the room tae the ither.

I want you to tell me the word you use for the following, she said, pointin at the class screen. *Not the 'correct' word, but the word you use among yourselves, in the playground.*

Someone who tells tales.

A grass.

Taking a day off school without permission.

Playing hookey.

A really wet day.

Miserable?

* * *

As they tellt her the words she typed them intae her laptop and they appeared as if by magic on the wall behind her.

OK – now how many of you have heard the word 'clype'?

Wan laddie put his haund up. *My granny says that.*

And what does it mean?

A grass.

How about dreich?

Naebdy. They repeated it efter her, and they couldnae even pronounce the ch sound – said dreak.

Then Gemma got them tae copy a list of words and look them up in a Scots dictionary.

Fankle, scunner, wheesht, midden, gloamin.

Ah went round the class, helpin them pronounce the words maistly. They were all brilliant at the computers, flingers fleein round the keyboards. Bright and shiny and articulate.

Then Gemma put a question on the screen.

Where were your parents born?

She collated the answers and her computer turnt them intae a big pie chart, the countries sliced intae it. Only thirty percent had two parents born in Scotland. Croatia, Bosnia, Pakistan, Hong Kong, US, England, Wales, Germany, Malaysia . . . the list went on.

What languages are spoken/have been spoken in your family?

Ah expected the chart tae be like the wan for the countries, but it wasnae. English, English, English – wan lassie said her mother spoke Italian and another had a granny that spoke Gaelic – *but only when she's on the phone to her brother, miss.*

Gemma looked round them. *Are we getting this right, here? Kuldip, does your mother not speak Urdu at home?*

No, miss.

Is there anyone whose family sometimes uses another language at home? Surely some of your parents want you to be bilingual?

What's that?

Speaking more than one language.

A hand went up. A wee lassie wi freckles.

Yes, Keri.

French.

You have family links to France?

No, but my mum and dad speak French with us sometimes to help me with my homework.

That wasn't quite what I meant. Didn't you say your parents came here from Bosnia?

But they speak English, now. We all speak English.

Another laddie pit his haund up.

My mother says it's better to speak English all the time, that if they still spoke their own language at home it'd confuse us. We're in Scotland now – we must speak the language of Scotland.

Which is . . .

English.

Is that the only language in Scotland?

Gaelic.

And what about when Mr McKeown comes in to talk to you, what is it he speaks?

Slang.

Does he?

Yeah.

The bell went and ah think it was just as well; ah could hear an edge tae her voice ah'd no heard afore. The perfect teacher control was slippin though the weans hadnae spotted it. They packed up cheerily and heided aff tae the dinner school (Student Refreshment Centre) leavin us in the empty classroom.

I didn't really expect that, she said.

What did you expect?

Dunno. . . . I was really pleased there were so many different places of origin – I expected there'd be loads of languages too. I think I hoped they'd open up a bit, that we'd be able to share more.

What is there tae share? When ah was wee ah lived next door tae a laddie whose granny was Polish and he didnae speak Polish.

It's such a waste. All that culture, that heritage and they let it go, don't even know they're losing it. They're turning into Americans. Gee, it's so cool.

You sound angry.

Scunnered. When I sat in on your class yesterday, it was like hearing my daddy.

But you don't sound like that.

I know. Maybe that's why I'm so mad. My mum was desperate for us to get on, go to uni, get a good job so we had to lose the accent, speak properly. My da was a quiet man, worked in the yards till everything fell apart and he was made redundant. He let her get on with making the decisions. He did the practical stuff, made me a hutch for the rabbit, fixed my bike. And every night he'd come into my room and give me a goodnight kiss, say 'Coorie doon, wee lass, coorie doon.'

She started tae move round the room, pushin chairs in under the desks.

He died last year. And I feel as if he's been lost – none of his children have become part of who he was. I look at these kids in the classroom denying their roots and I see myself. But I'm old enough to know what I've lost.

Well, mibbe your project'll help them see it a bit clearer. You never know – some of them might go hame and ask their parents tae teach them their ain language.

You wish.

Look ah better go – let you get on.

Ah knew she was gonnae greet and ah didnae want tae embarrass her. And there was nothin ah could dae – ah couldnae pit ma airm round her and tell her tae coorie in.

Ah walked through the playground on ma way oot. Weans joukin aboot, wee yins playin chasies, big yins hingin round, just like we were at that age, except there's nae smokers hidin round the back noo – they all get inoculated against it when they're eight – if they have so much as a puff they throw up.

In a way she was right – they are lossin somethin, though ah don't know if ah'd call it a culture. When ah was growin up ah didnae know ah had a culture, thought culture was opera and ballet dancin and nothin tae dae wi me. And history was Henry VIII or 1066, no the stuff ma parents and grandparents had done; leavin Ireland, gettin crap jobs in buildin sites and shipyerds and strugglin all their lives so the next generation wouldnae have tae. Probably some of ma faimly spoke Irish then, and ah speak a language ah didnae even know was a language tae some professor decided it was dyin oot and needed resuscitated. Does it matter if the weans don't know Urdu or Croatian? Will they turn round when they're thirty or forty and wish their parents had made them learn it? Mibbe they will but noo they're just weans.

When ah was a wean the school corridors were grey and we sat at scratched widden desks, starin oot the windaes wishin for four o clock when we could get oot and escape, play footie wi a tin can or a tennis ball. And even though we knew nothin aboot wer history or wer culture, the weight of wer parents laid heavy on wer shooders; unspoken darknesses. The piece and jam that kept yer belly fae rumblin at night, the boils on yer da's neck fae collars that could never be kept really clean, the wee wans that died of scarlet fever, penny insurance that made sure ye were buried respectably. It's still in wer blood and banes.

These weans shrug aff their parents' lives like last season's replica shirt. Even the wans whose faimlies have come here fae places of war, or famine or torture don't seem tae haud it in their bright eyes, their strong bodies, their high fives. Their classrooms are warm and bright, nae chalk dust driftin across the flair or the smell of wet anoraks steamin on radiators.

And as for wee Gemma; mibbe she has lost her daddy's voice and mibbe that's sad. But mibbe he's there in her spirit, in the way she makes that classroom alive, challenges them tae look ootside and inside.

At the school gate a tartan badge was lyin, fallen aff someone's fleece; the pin was bent and didnae work. Ah picked it up, rubbed it against ma jacket, then pit it in ma pocket, and walked on.

The state of Scotland

The state is proportionally larger in Scotland than the UK as a whole, both as an employer and spender of public money. So the role of the state in Scotland is clearly an important long-term issue. But a Scotland 2020 conference in Alloa showed that thinking about individual users' experiences of public services is at least as important as the size of the state.

The state of Scotland

The state is proportionally larger in Scotland than the UK as a whole, both as an employer and spender of public money. So the role of the state in Scotland is clearly an important long-term issue. But a Scotland 2020 conference in Alloa showed that thinking about individual users' experiences of public services is at least as important as the size of the state.

9. An Adaptive State

The personalisation of public services

One of the biggest issues facing the future of Scotland is the role of the public sector. In public debates in Scotland, this often focuses on whether the public sector is 'too big' or 'too inflexible', rather than on an examination of such areas as the culture, codes and internal and external environments in which organisations operate. An emerging theme in looking at innovative public sector practice is the idea of personalisation of services, which has been championed by Demos and Charlie Leadbeater, whose work in the area and Demos pamphlet, *Personalisation Through Participation: a new script for public services*, has framed much of the debate. As part of the Scotland 2020 programme, Demos held an event entitled 'An adaptive state', looking further at issues of public sector reform.

The future of Scotland's public services emerged as a critical issue in the Scotland 2020 scenarios workshops. The fact that the public sector spends more of GDP and employs more people proportionally than the UK as a whole proves its importance in any debate about Scotland's future.

The debate about the public sector tends to polarise views. One view is that a large state stifles entrepreneurialism, while the counter-argument is that market-based reforms in the public sector create inequalities.

We wanted to find a way to discuss reform of the public sector in Scotland that would avoid this polarisation. We decided to focus on the issue of personalisation, which has become a key concept in the public service reform debate. In a series of speeches during the year, Tony Blair and Gordon Brown talked about personalisation.

Brown made it clear that he does not see the idea as a form of quasi-privatisation:

> *Personalised services [are] not just for the few, for those who can afford to buy them in the market. . . . Personalisation is not opposed to equity; it is at the very core of what equity means. . . . Enabling each person to achieve their own potential to the fullest requires a tailored approach that takes into account each person's unique circumstances.*[1]

Demos associate Charles Leadbeater has argued that rather than trying to deliver existing services more efficiently, the aim of public service reform should be a different form of organisation, which would be able to adapt to the changing needs of users. In his short pamphlet, *Personalisation Through Participation*, Leadbeater described personalisation as follows:

> *Personalisation has the potential to reorganise the way we create public goods and deliver public services. But to unlock that potential the idea needs to be taken much further than current government thinking seems to allow.*
>
> *At the moment personalisation seems to mean providing better access and some limited say for users over how existing services are provided in largely traditional ways. This 'shallow' personalisation offers modest modification of mass produced, standardised services to partially adapt them to user needs.*
>
> *'Deep' personalisation would give users a far greater role – and also far greater responsibilities – for designing solutions from the ground up. . . . It could mean promoting greater capacity for self-management and self-organisation.*

Personalisation could be a sustaining innovation designed to make existing systems more personalised or it could be a disruptive innovation designed to put the users in the driving seat as designers and paymasters of services. It could be a programme to apply a lick of new paint to fading public services or it could be the harbinger of entirely new organisational logic.

'Scotland 2020: an adaptive state' was a one-day conference that brought together senior managers from public sector organisations, including local government, policing, health and the voluntary sector. The keynote session featured John Elvidge, permanent secretary at the Scottish Executive, talking about ways to make the public sector in Scotland more responsive to users' needs. An extract of this conversation is produced here.

In a session facilitated by Charlie Leadbeater, the conference also heard about two innovative public service initiatives in Glasgow that are putting personalisation into practice – the Sandyford Initiative, which has revolutionised the provision of sexual health care and advice and the Real network, an initiative to support lifelong learning in the city libraries. Short summaries of the projects are included here.

'Scotland 2020: an adaptive state' was held in Alloa on 26 October 2004 and was organised in partnership with Clackmannanshire Council. We would like to thank the council and all the staff at Gean House for making the event a success.

Notes

1   From the speech given by G Brown at the Social Market Foundation to launch the publication of his lecture 'A modern agenda for prosperity and social reform', 18 May 2004 (see www.smf.co.uk).

10. Public Sector Change

A conversation between
Iain Macwhirter and John Elvidge

Iain: It is my privilege to introduce John Elvidge, Permanent Secretary of the Scottish Executive, who is well known as a leading public service reformer. He has not had a huge amount of time probably to think about the reform agenda over the last couple of years thanks to events, and in particular the Holyrood Building Project.

However, as a result possibly of that experience he finds himself in a position where he has a commitment to root and branch reform of the Scottish Executive. We are going to talk about the extent to which some of the ideas discussed at the Demos Adaptive Scotland event could inform this reform agenda. And what these ideas mean to people who are actually going to be in the front line. So to start with – what does this reform mean to you and does it apply to Scotland?

John: I do not see the ideas that Charlie Leadbeater talked about as having any national boundaries around them. You either believe in customer-focused public services and personalisation and by extension co-production or you do not. It is a view of public services that probably divides people working in the public services more than it divides countries. Much of the work that we have been engaged with over the last while as an organisation has been to grapple with a set of cultural issues.

The grappling does not start from our point of view with the question: 'how do we deliver personalised public services?' The grappling starts with the questions: 'what's the role of government within the vision that people have for post-devolution Scotland? what do the aspirations that people have for post-devolution Scotland imply for the kind of government that they want?' One of my fundamental beliefs is that people should always ask themselves what they can do to move towards the solutions before they ask what other people can do.

Iain: Do you think there was a coherent public expectation of what devolution would deliver in terms of the public services?

John: I think that there was a very clear belief that devolution would deliver an improved quality of life across a broad spectrum of people's contact with the public sector. It was partly that sense of outcomes and partly that the nature of people's relationship with the state would be different post-devolution. It was not a purely managerialist solution. There was something about people's perceptions of themselves as citizens which was also a part of the vision, but (to borrow one of Charlie's thoughts) it isn't reasonable to expect people who have those aspirations to be responsible for translating it into a vision of government.

That would be placing a demand on people to articulate a set of solutions which it simply isn't fair to place on them. I think people have got to have the right to set the tests and that as professionals we have to accept the obligation of finding ways of meeting the tests. Anyway that was our starting point. Three and a half years into devolution we thought that it would be a good idea to ask various sets of people how they thought we as an organisation were getting on with this process. So we asked a number of stakeholders, ministers and the people who work in the organisation how they thought we had done in the journey into the first few years of devolution.

Iain: What did they think of it so far?

John: The answers were remarkably consistent. The organisation had achieved a lot of difficult things in transition. We could do with a bit of international perspective here, as people around the world are astonished that the UK could manage a series of constitutional changes of such magnitude. And do so without a breakdown of public services and/or a breakdown of public order, disturbances on the street, or any visible discontinuity in the delivery of public services. So by and large people were saying 'yes – you did the not dropping the ball bit very well.' They also said that this is not enough. Beyond not dropping the ball – a necessary step – you have a distance to go towards fulfilling our aspiration of being a different kind of organisation for a different political and constitutional context. And hopefully they gave us some clues of what that direction of travel might look like.

Those clues were essentially about cultural issues. I think I would say, people saw us as not yet a participative organisation in the way that we did business. Words such as 'arrogance' crept into people's descriptions of their experience of working with us and people said things, not just about our unwillingness to be partners with them. They implied that we might not be their partner of choice, either, and that if this were a dance, we might be the person left standing at the side of the room. They also said that they thought our vision of our responsibilities was too limited. They recognised that there was a series of things that we had traditionally done around policy-making, that we were unsurprisingly quite good at – having spent several decades practising being quite good at it. But they thought that that was too limited a vision of what government should be.

What we needed, it was felt, was to see a role for ourselves that came further down the chain towards outcomes. One of the distinguishing features of the organisation that people recognise is that we do not in essence provide direct public-service delivery to the citizen: our responsibilities by and large stop further up the chain between government and citizen. They thought that we tended to take the job to a certain point and then say to local authorities or health boards or whatever, 'well then off you go – over to you now – we've done our bit.'

Iain: One impression of what's happened since devolution is that you have some competition with politicians/ministers doing what they're doing, and being unsure about their powers and how they want to use them. And in a sense the Executive have been caught in the middle there because of the expectations that the politicians are trying to respond to and the lack of powers to meet them with.

John: There is a debate about lack of powers, certainly, but it seems to me that people have been perhaps reluctant to recognise that devolution is and was a learning process for everybody. It seems to me an unreasonable expectation that ministers were going to spring fully formed into an understanding of how best to contribute. There would have been something contrary to the spirit of devolution if ministers on day one had said 'we have a complete set of answers to all this' without allowing relationships and attitudes to evolve and emerge.

I think given what I said about the expectations of devolution it seems to me natural that there should have been systematic re-examination of every area of public life, to ask the fundamental questions: 'are we trying to achieve the right things? are we going about it the right way?' I don't think it is fundamentally surprising that people should experience a sense of upheaval everywhere, at once.

Iain: Is this part of the learning process?

John: Yes – and part of responding to expectations. Something I particularly wanted to say, just picking one area: education. One of the first pieces of legislation that Parliament passed was the first major piece of education legislation that we have had in Scotland for a long time. At its heart was a fundamentally radical statement of the relationship between the citizen and the state in the context of education. It was the first time we have created an obligation on the state to meet the educational needs of every individual child. Previously our legislation, like the legislation that still currently exists in England, was to deliver a product called education to consumers, and if there wasn't a match between that product and the individual child, well that was not a breach of the statutory obligation.

Under the statutory framework that Parliament created in 2000 that model was fundamentally changed to create a legal obligation to maximise the potential of the individual child. A hugely difficult statutory standard to meet, but a good example of putting personalisation right at the heart of one's concept of the system. I am not going to sit here and pretend that we have managed to find the right way of expressing that concept in every other policy field post-devolution. What I would argue is that this is one of the reasons why we shouldn't be too dismissive of the process of review and reconsideration that's followed devolution.

Iain: The public sector certainly has a very bad image at the moment in certain parts of this country. This is a difficult question, and one filled with all kinds of complexities but, overall, in the round, do you think the public sector is too big in Scotland?

John: This is a tricky question. There are two ways of answering that question. Is 27 per cent of the workforce too many people to employ in delivery of the public services? Well not so evidently so. There is an important argument for Scotland about how economic growth is to be supported within our static population (and potentially a declining population of working age) and if the public sector is at risk of taking too much talent out of the employment pool, and thereby endangering economic growth. I think that the answer has to be not by any automatic arithmetic principle. One simply has to observe that there may be increasing competition for talent inside the Scottish labour market.

But there's another issue, which is the proportion of GDP we spend on public services – it's 51 per cent, one of the highest levels in the world. And it is difficult for countries to afford that level of redirection of wealth into public services. Not technically difficult but it raises issues of public consent and the distribution of wealth. The fact that we are at one extreme of the world distribution has to cause us to ask some questions and the First Minister has publicly raised concerns about this issue. It's not as simplistic as saying 'it must be wrong' but whenever you're out at one end of a distribution you do have to say to yourself 'am I sure that this is the right place to be?' So there's certainly a question to be asked about the proportion of our wealth that we channel in that way.

Iain: That is one of the questions clearly being asked by the First Minister Jack McConnell, and his answer to it is to cut public spending in Scotland more than is being cut south of the border by Gordon Brown. How much of a culture change is that going to involve – out-Gershoning Gershon?

John: If I can be bureaucratically precise for a moment, the First Minister is not trying to cut the level of public expenditure. What he is trying to cut is the proportion of public expenditure that goes into administering public services as opposed to the proportion of public expenditure that goes into supplying public services. The objective is that by redistributing resources towards the delivery it should make delivery better, and if one believes that there's a correlation between resources and the quality of delivery then it must achieve that result. I appreciate that believing that there's a direct correlation between the level of resources and the quality of delivery is a complex question, but in principle it creates the conditions that the quality of delivery can get better.

Is it challenging? Will it change the shape of things? Well, it is hard to say. There's a debate about whether Scotland has advantages as a country, or the size we are, relative to a country the size of England. It may be there are efficiencies in running the public sector that are available to a country of five million people that are not available to a country of 50 million plus people. And that there may be solutions that are more readily within our grasp than is the case in England. Normally when I am talking Scotland up to non-Scottish audiences, I pick out some examples of ways in which we're already doing that. We have constructed a new procurement system which is capable of covering the whole of the public sector, and which the *Financial Times* described as a world leader in new procurement models. Much of the debate in the south about efficiency is about the fact that within central government there's a multiplicity of different systems. That's simply not true in Scotland. That shift to having one set of systems that supports all the business of central government is a step we took a decade ago.

Iain: As you know, some parts of the public sector such as certain strands of local government are a bit sceptical here. Some of them think that the Executive is trying to get them to bear the burden of cutting the state to meet these kinds of targets, which many of them think are unrealisable.

John: I suppose that one of the things I would want to say is that ministers took care to impose a more demanding year-on-year reduction target on the Executive than they imposed on other public bodies. So this was not an exercise in asking other bits of the public sector to do things that we weren't prepared to do ourselves. That does not detract from the fact that what we're trying to do is challenging for everybody. But I don't think it helps us in the challenge that we have to argue about whether any of us is trying to duck out of the challenge. Because the answers to the challenge are about cooperating with each other; therefore falling out would not be a good start.

Iain: I am sure that Charles Leadbeater would be a little concerned at the drift of this conversation. We are going right down the old top-down target approach, and we should be looking at it more bottom up. This target culture happened because there's been a collapse of trust in politicians and the political process, and politicians tried to respond to this by creating the target culture, which has not restored trust. To what extent do you think that these ideas about personalising public services are possible, given this kind of media and wider public climate?

John: I think we need to go through some pain in relation to the issue of trust, to achieve it. When you step from one place to another place you cannot demonstrate that a different way of delivering public services will work until you've gone there and done it. You go through a trust barrier and at a time of low trust in government at all levels and government in all places, there's nothing unique about Scotland. Making the kind of step that demands huge trust from the citizen is inherently a challenging thing to do. Particularly since we're all recognising that it's not very easy to make the new model work in an instantaneous way, because it depends often on the patterns of cooperation between public bodies. And those patterns take time to become established and time to work.

We are seeing that in a sense with the community planning process which many people in the room might argue is our attempt to create a set of frameworks that ought to help us with some of the challenges. It is going to be hugely difficult, because getting people to work together is challenging at a day-to-day delivery level but getting the consent of the citizens to make that step to a different model is also challenging in its own way.

Iain: Given this idea of personalised services, one of the dilemmas it seems to me is that sometimes what people want might well conflict with what is the most rational allocation or use of resources. I am thinking here of the hospital closures campaign which is running across Scotland, has got MPs and MSPs panicking about their seats and seems to be leading to a number of concessions in different areas of the country. I just wonder if that's something that you think about yourself – the problem of reconciling rational administration of the public sector with what people's demands are at local level? Once they do get involved! If they get involved!

John: I always start from the proposition that if something's right, it must be possible to build public understanding and support for that thing. I know that's not a straightforward process but I think you have to believe that that's possible because otherwise it seems to me that one is not trusting people to exercise the kind of participative role that we have talked about today. I think openness is probably the key here. The hospitals issue seems to me a classic 'I wouldn't start from here' proposition. What has evolved is an acute conflict between what people think is the model of health delivery that is in their best interests, and what the professional view of the model of delivery is. This conflict has emerged because there has not been sufficient sharing of understanding of the issues before the point of articulating solutions. And this contains a wider lesson for all of us in public life and public service – about the need for greater communication and dialogue, and the fact that we have to make difficult choices.

Iain Macwhirter is a political commentator for the Herald *and* Sunday Herald *and presenter of BBC Scotland's* Politics Scotland *and* Holyrood Live *programmes. John Elvidge is Permanent Secretary to the Scottish Executive.*

11. The Sandyford Initiative

Innovation in practice – a revolution in the provision of sexual health care and advice

Alison Bigrigg

The Sandyford Initiative is a sexual, reproductive and emotional health service formed in 2001 by the amalgamation of hospital-based Genitourinary Medicine, community Family Planning services and the multi-agency Centre for Women's Health. It is funded by Greater Glasgow NHS Board and located in the centre of Glasgow, with a range of projects and services in community sites across the city.

It has around 200 staff, a budget of £6 million per annum and over 100,000 client–patient contacts per year. This is not a small project with hand-picked workers, but a significant unit with staff ranging from consultants and counsellors to librarians. In 2001, staff attitudes to work and clients reflected the environment in which they worked, separate traditions and professions, and the training they had undergone. New members of staff now frequently comment favourably on the enthusiasm and passion they find in Sandyford showing that although it demands a personalised approach to public service, this can be rewarding to staff as well as clients.

When the Sandyford Initiative was formed, the majority of staff agreed to three basic principles focusing on individuals or groups of users, as follows.

O   An individual's health is determined not only by the
     presence or absence of disease, but also by social aspects
     of their past and present lives and those around them.

O   All groups in society do not have equal access to health
    care and there is a need to reduce these inequalities as well
    as to improve access for all.
O   Services need to be designed by and for their users.

From the medical to the social: the Sandyford Health Screen

The first of these principles was put into practice by developing an integrated model of health giving equal importance to medical and social models. The medical model of health is a traditional approach taught and practised by all clinicians. This involves taking a detailed account of the patient's presenting symptoms and past illnesses, operations, etc. The social model looks at the patient's current concerns, past and present social experiences, such as the influence of alcohol, poverty and violence, and considers how their health and social needs can be more broadly addressed.

Structured pro forma for history-taking are commonplace in health services. They are used to ensure there is a consistent approach to individual patients. When the Sandyford Initiative was formed, each clinical service was using a medical pro forma for new clients. The new service developed a structural pro forma to ask about social factors, which became known as 'The Sandyford Health Screen'.

This raised many factors that clinicians could not solve, but which have a direct effect on an individual's health, such as sexual abuse, domestic violence, bullying and so forth. What started as a separate medical and social pro forma was quickly merged into one based on the experience of frontline staff.

Routine use of this tool has led to clinicians working much closer with counsellors, librarians and other non-clinical staff. Mutual respect and understanding has developed, followed by a true appreciation of why information and client–patient self-determination are fundamental to improvements in long-term health. This is reflected in the current Sandyford structure where services are presented not according to traditional medical discipline, but in terms of whether individuals are presenting with symptoms of ill health or seeking to improve and protect their sexual, reproductive and emotional health.

The second basic principle on which the Sandyford Initiative was created was the need to reduce barriers to access. This was founded on the belief that to achieve a healthy society, people need access to health information, emotional support and advice, and services both to attain and also to maintain good health. This is far removed from a culture that puts up barriers to access to prevent waiting lists growing and hence, failure to achieve centrally imposed targets.

The Sandyford Initiative, therefore, provides direct access appointments during the day and evening, but also has a walk-in service every morning for those who need immediate support with sexual and reproductive needs. This guarantees that if you arrive before 10am you may have to wait, but you will be seen. One hundred to 200 individuals attend this service every day.

Furthermore, Sandyford recognises that there are some groups in society who find it harder to access services and who may benefit from these services being tailored for their particular needs. In Sandyford, numerous services have been and will be designed around needs as they are identified from community participation, analysis of Sandyford Health Screen statistics or good practice elsewhere. Examples of such services include:

O   a walk-in service 4–6pm Monday to Thursday and
     Saturday afternoons for teenagers
O   late evening services in the red light district for prostitutes
O   a dedicated service for gay men and men who have sex
     with men
O   outreach and fast-track in-reach for the homeless.

From market segmentation to self-identification

The development of dedicated services for specific groups in the population can sometimes be regarded as segmentation and has not always been popular. The difference from many models is that, at Sandyford, individuals choose how or if they wish to identify themselves. The user selects the service they attend, for example one-third of gay men with sexually transmitted infections choose the generic sexually transmitted infection service and two-thirds choose the one advertised specifically for gay men. Users move from one service to another as they wish, and no one is labelled or defined by the service providers. Wherever users access the service, the core medical treatment will be the same and of the highest quality, but the opening hours, appointment system, waiting room environment, volunteers, host helpers, partner agencies present, staffing mix and information presented will all be different.

Development of such tailored services is a natural extension of personalisation. When users identify common requirements, services should respond to these needs. The individual must retain the right to choose which service he or she uses. Services in turn need to be flexible enough to respond to this demand while ensuring they are always exploring unmet needs in other areas, both in terms of other population groups and other core services. The Sandyford Initiative demonstrates that this vision – one of an evolving, learning, listening organisation, adapting and changing to its environment and the needs of clients – is possible and one with wider implications for health services and the public sector.

The third core principle on which the Sandyford Initiative was built was that user involvement is central to the core of service reform. Sexual health is an area where it is traditionally regarded as difficult or impossible to involve users. The Sandyford has no magical wand, but shows it is possible, if service leaders are determined and prioritise the principle. Sandyford employs common techniques including comment cards, self-administered questionnaires, focus groups, user groups, stakeholder groups and one-to-one interviews. An experienced member of staff has the full-time remit of coordinating user and potential user input into the service and of encouraging all staff to see this as central to their way of working. The methods used are tailored to the needs of the individual or groups. For example, Sandyford has a well-established stakeholders' group for lesbian, gay, bisexual and transgendered service users, as this community has a number of organisations that are well established, but when consulting young people will tend to use short-term groups concentrating on one project.

Focusing on the needs of users has led Sandyford into providing services with more emphasis on factors underlying initial presentation, information provision and user empowerment. It has also demonstrated the need for partnership and collaborative approaches. Sandyford has shown this can be achieved, even in an area so riddled with controversy and value-laden judgement as sexual and reproductive health (and particularly so in parts of Scotland).

The question arises as to whether a new unit is required to produce such change; this is unlikely as service reorganisations can be a negative and time-diverting activity, as well as a stimulus for change. There is a need, however, for energetic and passionate leadership to create a sense of something new and important where change, as long it is focused on the needs of individual users or potential users, is welcomed.

Sandyford shows the potential of developing new ways of working, new models, organisations and culture, as well as new types of advocacy and leadership. It contains wider implications for the public sector reform debate – showing that one can develop a different model from the traditional ones of producer capture on the one side and marketisation on the other. Sandyford is about the emergence of a new ethos – shaped by personalisation, collaboration and a sense of co-ownership. Our journey has only begun, but in an external climate shaped by Scotland's appalling public health record, numerous sexual health challenges, and a nervousness in parts of Scotland on issues of sex, sexuality and the body, Sandyford has made startling progress in a relatively short period.

Further information about the Sandyford Initiative may be found at *www.sandyford.org*

Alison Bigrigg has been director of the Sandyford Initiative since it was established in 2001.

12. The Learning Network

The Real experience – a move towards lifelong learning

Jonathan Clark

During 1998 the Glasgow Development Agency (GDA) established the Learning Inquiry which aimed to help transform Glasgow's learning landscape. Its purpose was to generate practical solutions, dissolve barriers to learning and enable Glasgow to transform itself into a 'Learning City'. The Inquiry was set up to deal with four main points:

○ how to get more organisations involved in developing their people
○ how to stimulate personal motivation to learn
○ how to surmount the barriers to learning
○ how to encourage institutions to improve quality in the supply of and access to learning and how such achievement is evaluated.

As Stuart Gulliver, former chief executive officer of the GDA noted at the launch:

> *Lifelong learning is a challenge we cannot afford to duck. Glasgow's future success depends on our engagement. We have our problems but the good news is coming in; we are as well placed as we have been for 25 years. We mean Glasgow to become a Learning City and have set the target of 100,000 new learners; it is our aim to achieve that target as fast as we can.*

One of the principal outcomes of the process was the development of the Real Partnership.

The Partnership developed following a meeting of the main public sector stakeholders in August 1999 to explore possibilities for joint working in the development of a physical and virtual network to support lifelong learning in the city. In the weeks and months after the meeting a consensus emerged that there should be greater collaboration and unity of purpose to ensure that the city derived the maximum benefit from the various investments being made at that time.

In April 2000 the first Real learning centre was opened in Ibrox library on the south side of the city. It marked a significant point since this was the first development under the Real brand. As the Rt Hon. Donald Dewar, the then First Minister noted at the launch:

> *In Glasgow, this vision is being taken forward by a unique partnership which spans further and higher education, local government and the Scottish Enterprise Network. This partnership aims to transform Glasgow into one of Europe's Learning Cities, where first class education and training resources are developed to release the potential of local people.*

Development of the brand had followed on from research into attitudes and behaviours towards learning carried out during 1998/99 under the auspices of the Learning Inquiry. It was clear that establishing a brand was important not only from the customers' perspective, but also from that of the partners. For customers, the brand signalled a level of quality and also better integration of services. For partners, the brand provided a 'neutral' space to collaborate, and a sense of common purpose.

Over time partners in the city, including the council, further and higher education and the private sector, have adopted the brand and applied it to physical locations, online resources and in the promotion of various products and services. Glasgow remains unique

Figure 1 Growth in membership 2001–04

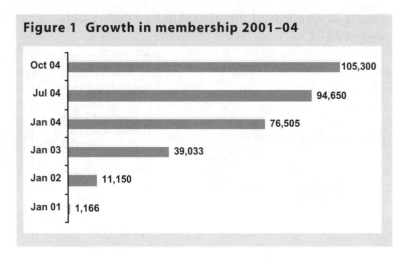

Oct 04	105,300
Jul 04	94,650
Jan 04	76,505
Jan 03	39,033
Jan 02	11,150
Jan 01	1,166

in having an active partnership with a variety of organisations collaborating under a common banner.

Since 1999 the partnership has focused on four interrelated areas:

○ the development of the physical environment
○ the development of digital resources and infrastructure
○ the development of learning projects
○ the development of the partnership.

In less than five years the membership of Real has grown to some 105,000, while user figures are considerably higher (see figure 1). No money has been spent on advertising. Word of mouth has been the primary vehicle for marketing the project and its services. Evaluations and research carried out during 2003/04 showed that Real is reaching across the city not only in terms of geography, but also in terms of age and socioeconomic backgrounds (see figure 2). This reflects the approach of the partnership in not adopting a 'deficit' model of learning.

Looking to the future – true learning cities of the twenty-first century will have to move beyond the formal education and training

Figure 2 Analysis of membership by employment status 2003

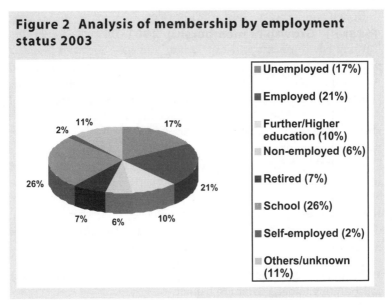

- Unemployed (17%)
- Employed (21%)
- Further/Higher education (10%)
- Non-employed (6%)
- Retired (7%)
- School (26%)
- Self-employed (2%)
- Others/unknown (11%)

systems based on a 'metronomic' curriculum delivered primarily through instruction towards more flexible, non-linear approaches that build capabilities as well as competencies. Learning has to be self-motivated since policy or legislation cannot prescribe it to the unwilling. Understanding the power of intrinsic motivation will help to develop experiences that attract significantly larger numbers of people in learning and sustain their engagement over their lifetime without compulsion.

Future learning systems will have to embed the delivery of learning within the context of people's lives more effectively – within the workplace, home and community. These contexts fall outwith the boundaries of formal education and the remit of many statutory institutions. Despite the emergence of the experience economy, the design of learning systems, resources and environments remains largely unchallenged and unchanged. How many of today's learning experiences live on in people's imaginations and generate emotions of excitement, curiosity and fun?

Design will increasingly play a key role in the process of creating new ways of collaborative learning and knowledge exchange. Future learning environments and experiences will have to blend together physical and virtual spaces, fostering the creation of social relationships and networks that are fluid and distributed. The situation of learning within the non-linear and complex realities of people's lives will be aided by the availability of technology, but will also require good design and the fusion of different creative perspectives ranging from the arts to business.

In a world where human performance has been identified as the most important strategic factor by three-quarters of executives world-wide (ahead of productivity and technology), the availability of effective and efficient learning systems will become an ever-increasing priority for individuals, businesses and cities. The challenge is for public sector learning provision to be truly adaptive.

Jonathan Clark works for Scottish Enterprise Glasgow and is involved in the development of the Real network.

Where are we headed?

The future will be shaped by the complex and unpredictable interaction of social, political and economic forces. We asked experts on the key trends to consider the future of Scotland. What will happen after Barnett? Can Dundee become a biotech and cultural capital? Should we democratise football? And what place should Scotland take in Europe and the world?

13. Boho Boffins

Why cities need science and jazz

Melissa Mean

Dundee has a world-class cancer research cluster but, despite several positive developments, it can hardly claim to be a cultural capital. Will this hamper the city's ability to attract world-class talent?

Cities are back. After almost three decades of headlines announcing the death and decline of cities, in the early to mid 1990s a new activity has emerged: resurgent city-spotting. Journalists from *Conde Nast, Wallpaper Navigator** and *The Sunday Times* style magazine are being kept busy concocting lists of the latest centres of urban cool. The current front-runners include Cairo, Copenhagen, Glasgow, London, Sao Paulo, Sapporo and Shanghai.

There are a number of competing story lines behind the headlines that try to explain the return of cities. One of the most common is culture-led regeneration, originally scripted by the likes of Gateshead and Bilbao, but galleries and icon architecture are now the main characters in regeneration strategies everywhere from LA to Slough. Another story line tells of the power of clusters and comes from the gospel of Harvard professor Michael Porter, whose theory of economic growth powered by interconnected firms has been applied to cities. A third popular story is about the rise of the weightless knowledge-economy, anchored down in cities by research universities and creative industries.

However, there is a danger that as these stories get repeated and re-used, they've become clichés, uprooted from their context, and in the process losing their power to explain or engage people. So is there still real substance in these stories and can they provide any pointers for where next?

This paper looks at the broad changes affecting cities and the challenges and questions for a city like Dundee. To build sustainable creative urban ecologies, world-class science labs and a vibrant jazz scene are helpful, but they're not the whole story.

The return of cities can only be explained in the context of the rise of the creative age – a long wave of change affecting every sector of the economy, in which competitiveness and wealth have become increasingly determined by the capacity for innovation and creativity. The contrast with the industrial age could not be sharper, as Fredrick Taylor, the American industrial engineer, made brutally clear a hundred years ago: 'Individual insight is an impediment in the Industrial Age. A good worker is merely a man more or less of the type of an ox, heavy both mentally and physically. Man can become no more than a veritable machine.'[1]

We have moved from an age of mass reproduction where you could have any colour as long as it's black, to an age of mass personalisation and mass customisation. This new pattern of production and growth increasingly depends on an open-ended process of cooperation and collaboration between many different players with tight feedback loops between firms, organisations, suppliers, customers, marketers and the broader environment.

Proximity and diversity

Cities matter in the creative age because, at their best, they provide a platform that is well suited to supporting and nourishing this new growth pattern. This capability is predicated on two key qualities: proximity and diversity.

Cities provide key nodes for the circulation and exchange of people, ideas and innovations. Wireless communication, the internet and faster and cheaper air travel have not only not lessened the importance of proximity and face-to-face contacts, but even seem to encourage it, increasing the magnetic power and stickiness of some places to attract and retain people.

The importance of proximity has been transformed from the industrial age, where what mattered was proximity to a port and a large fairly homogenous labour market, to the creative economy where what counts is proximity to a mix of markets, skills, clients, media, users and customers.

The value of proximity and the ability that it gives a city to re-wire and reshape itself become clear when it is considered that for every 1–2 per cent plus or minus in annual variation of overall number of jobs, roughly 15 per cent of the volume of jobs are created and destroyed during the same period.[2]

Diversity is vital because it is through combining and colliding new and old that innovation and adaptation occur. The more open a city is to new people, new ideas and new ways of living, the greater its creative metabolism will be. The American mathematician and software designer Eric Raymond explains this difference between open systems and closed systems through contrasting two models of development: the cathedral and the bazaar.[3]

Raymond was more interested in the most effective way to debug a computer program, but his analysis offers equal insight for city planners and policy-makers. A cathedral is typically designed by one architect or a small team, pressing hundreds of people into making the masterplan real. It is a slow and rigid development process, and allows little flexibility once completed.

In contrast the bazaar can appear in a vacant lot one afternoon and be knocked down the same evening. But the most successful result from years of community involvement and interactions between merchants, customers and others all making small and sometimes radical innovations and adjustments over time. The more people and the wider range of different types of people you can draw on to help your innovation process, the easier and more sustainable it is.

So, a city's very structure consists of its diversity and proximity – its mixture and mixing of uses – and we get closest to its structural secrets when we deal with the conditions that generate diversity and proximity. The spread over the last five years of the cluster as a must-have of any self-respecting urban regeneration strategy is very much an attempt to try and rebuild on a micro-scale the conditions of diversity and proximity that have been lost in cities through decades of zoning, separation of uses and centralist, command-and-control planning.

Micro-clusters and beyond

Almost every city has its own version of Birmingham's Custard Factory – a hub of media and arts industries piled into a hitherto redundant warehouse or the backrooms of an art gallery. However, fragmented micro-clusters can only carry a city so far. The challenge now for cities is to break creativity and diversity out of the cluster and embed it across the whole urban fabric.

Some patterns are now emerging that question our assumptions about which cities and regions are doing better at meeting this challenge. In a Demos report published this year, *Europe in the Creative Age*,[4] the US economist Richard Florida builds on his earlier work, *The Rise of the Creative Class*,[5] by comparing 14 EU countries with the US and ranking them according to how they score on the three Ts of creative competitiveness – talent, technology and tolerance.

Florida identifies the emergence of a creative crescent comprising Finland, Sweden, Denmark and the Netherlands. Moreover, this crescent is challenging the long assumed predominance of the US with Sweden knocking it off the number one spot. These Nordic countries successfully combine an intense, open and innovative enterprise culture with some of the most egalitarian social and civic cultures in the world.

In Florida's ranking, the UK lies just above mid table (there is unfortunately no breakdown for Scotland). Clearly this hides great differences between cities – the experiences of Manchester and Edinburgh contrast sharply with places like Sunderland and the twin city experience of growth and poverty found in Glasgow. It is important to remember that, within an overall national picture, historically outlier cities can move from nowhere to challenging for slots at the top of the premier city league. Michael Parkinson's recent report for the Core Cities Group evaluating European urban performance highlighted, for example, how Barcelona has done just that over the past ten years.[6]

Population decline

So what are the ingredients for renewal for Dundee? At the moment Dundee still looks like an outlier city. While Scotland's overall population is rising, Dundee's continues its 30-year decline – in the last ten years the city has lost 14,000 people with the under-45s in particular choosing to leave. Since 1995, employment in most sectors has been in decline and the unemployment rate is running at 6.3 per cent compared with a Scottish national average of 4.1 per cent. Dundee has also gained the dubious honour of having the highest teenage pregnancy rate in Scotland, with the Dundee East parliamentary constituency having a rate of 7.4 per cent.

More importantly, Dundee captures the contradictions of much of modern life in a medium-sized town and city, with some groups enjoying a good life, fuelled by low property prices, allowing its small middle class to enjoy a high disposable income. In other areas, Dundee has a sense of an older, more static Scotland, seen in the description of Dundee by the writer Charles Jennings in his travelogue around Scotland, *Faintheart*, commenting that 'people were walking around in that tut-tutting way of middle-aged Scots.'[7]

If we look at issues of diversity in Dundee we find some common ground with this position. This is, like large parts of Scotland, a fairly un-multicultural place with little experience of black and ethnic minority immigration.

The strange paradox here is that while parts of Dundee are locked into older certainties, this ignores the waves of previous change that have informed and still carry ripples today. Dundee was the destination of significant Irish immigration to Scotland in the nineteenth and early twentieth centuries, encouraged by the growth of the jute industry. And the city was also significantly changed by the high number of women working in this sector, with unemployed men earning the name of 'kettle watchers' while they waited for their womenfolk to come home. These earlier waves of change have left marks upon Dundee's culture and psyche which are still visible today.

Future directions for Dundee

There are no silver bullets and no masterplans, but what follows is a set of questions or challenges that any city would do well to engage with if it wants to re-tool itself for the creative age effectively.

First, Dundee needs to avoid the increasingly commodified ideas and strategies for regeneration. A familiar formula has emerged: iconic gallery + loft apartments + university + creative cluster = urban renewal.

As Kate Oakley recently pointed out,[8] it's not that creativity and the knowledge economy aren't important, but the missing bit is about how those meta-trends impact upon and interact with the particular assets, capacities and needs of different and distinctive places. Gateshead's culture-led regeneration strategy was pioneering when the council began to work on it over 15 years ago; for any city today adopting such a strategy is little better than a simulacrum rather than the real thing.

The challenge is not to copy the last, increasingly spent, wave of innovative urban regeneration, but to mobilise resources around what could be a new wave. The competitive advantage of Dundee could be marshalled around ideas such as 'the best place in Scotland to bring up a child', or 'a great place for baby boomers to grow old'. To support either aspiration properly would require a comprehensive re-configuration of the city and its resources.

Second, by identifying tolerance as a pillar of economic competitiveness Florida highlights the importance of immaterial assets in creating successful cities. Northern Europe has historically fused high levels of tolerance and social trust with very homogeneous populations. Growing cultural and ethnic diversity act as benign spurs to innovation and creativity, but they also challenge established relationships.

If Dundee is to increase and then retain its openness in the context of an increasingly pluralised society, then new forms of trust will need to be developed. Moreover, there is an urgent need to move beyond our current limited conception of tolerance as mutual non-interference towards the more active creation of social trust. The approach to multiculturalism and anti-discrimination fashioned over the last two generations is ill-equipped for this task. A priority for all cities will be to develop and promote policies that reinforce this immaterial infrastructure, including shared values, cooperation and collective learning.

Third, creating favourable conditions to attract talent from outside needs to be twinned with nurturing and spreading home-grown talent. By offering the right kind of quality of place (open, diverse, accessible culture) Dundee could well prosper from America's current political environment which is restricting scientific research and making border entry harder: between 2001 and 2002 the number of US visas issued for foreign-born workers in science and technology fell by a staggering 55 per cent. However, to avoid the dangers of a two-speed city, Dundee must ensure home-grown creative potential is not wasted. A key challenge will be to achieve a better match between public education and the demands of a creative economy and society.

Fourth and finally, as highlighted above, the next challenge for a city like Dundee is to break creativity out of the cluster/art gallery/ science lab and integrate it with the rest of the city's activities and institutions. What is the creative agenda for Dundee's public services? Housing provision? Governance structures? Equally, discussions about the creative economy sometimes get limited to the Friday–Sunday city, but the Monday–Thursday city needs to work for people too if a sustainable quality of place and quality of life is to be created. One way to begin this process would be for Dundee's existing creative clusters – in its jazz scene and science research labs – to start talking and experiment with some inter-cluster collaboration.

If Dundee can successfully engage with these kinds of questions, then it will be well equipped with enough material to craft its own distinctive story rather than rely on second-hand and increasingly standardised formulas from other places.

Melissa Mean is head of the cities programme at Demos. A version of this paper was presented at a public debate on urban regeneration at Dundee Contemporary Arts (DCA), Dundee, on 20 May 2004. We would like to thank the DCA and Scottish Enterprise Tayside for their support.

Notes

1   FW Taylor, *The Principles of Scientific Management* (New York: Harper Bros, 1911).
2   P Veltz, 'The rationale for a resurgence in the major cities of advanced economies', paper presented at the Resurgent City conference, London School of Economics, 2004.
3   ES Raymond, *The Cathedral and the Bazaar* (Sebastopol, CA: O'Reilly, 2001).
4   R Florida and I Tinagli, *Europe in the Creative Age* (London: Demos, 2004).
5   R Florida, *The Rise of the Creative Class* (New York: Basic Books, 2002).
6   M Parkinson, M Hutchins, J Simmie et al, *Competitive European Cities: where do the core cities stand?* (London: Office of the Deputy Prime Minister, January 2004).
7   C Jennings, *Faintheart: an Englishman ventures north of the border* (London: Abacus, 2001).
8   K Oakley, 'Developing policy as a shared narrative' in T Bentley and J Wilsdon (eds), *The Adaptive State* (London: Demos, 2003).

14. The Age of Capitals
Edinburgh as Culture City

Marc Lambert

There are many Scotlands within Scotland. I wanted to capture the strangeness of the one I know.

Alan Warner

It is a lively time for scenario spinning in the arts. Jack McConnell outlined culture policy in his 2003 St Andrew's Day speech, and the tectonic plates have been shifting beneath the arts world ever since. So far the transition has not appeared a very happy one, with controversy over Scottish Opera and the National Theatre as evidence of recent bruises. And given the size of the task facing the government sponsored Cultural Commission, its problematic relationship with local authorities, and the uncertain history of cultural policy initiatives in general, one might be forgiven for feeling a bit pessimistic. Yet there's a strange sense of expectancy in the air. With the opening of the Scottish Parliament, and UNESCO's validation of Edinburgh as a City of Literature, the capital has once again moved centre stage as a place of action and recognition. To a greater extent matters are now in our own hands. There is an opportunity, despite our historic pessimism, for well-planned change and improvement in Scotland. Or am I being naive?

In this essay I want to put these recent developments in a wider historical and cultural context, touching on tensions which exist within some of the ideas we have about our own culture and where it should go. I argue that a critical examination of these ideas, and the stories they represent about ourselves and our history, is an essential element to every project which attempts through policy to script our future. This evaluation is necessary if we are to exorcise some of the ghosts that inhabit our thinking and hold us back from progressing beyond the normal default positions that we often take up. Scotland is not a nation short of critical self-evaluation, but it is seldom carried out in a helpful manner. Nor do we know anything like as much as we should about our own history and its contradictions and complexities. Hamish Henderson once wrote that 'As a nation we have . . . a past with which we haven't completely come to terms.'[1] On a proper investigation of that past we might be surprised by what we find.

As this is Edinburgh's day in the sun, I begin with some thoughts on the historical relationship of capital cities to the culture and nation they attempt to represent. I touch on the effect that the removal of executive power from the capital in 1707 had on the stories we then came to tell about our history and culture. I take examples from literature, noting that the romantic movement which swept Europe during this period was heavily indebted to MacPherson's Ossian and the works of Walter Scott (not to mention Byron). This connection between powerlessness and romanticism is no accident. It gives us the cult of landscape and the picturesque – what can easily be dismissed as chocolate box history. Yet, however romantically, writers like Scott did articulate something fundamentally important about a threatened identity and its history, culture and politics. And an echo of this urge, albeit expressed in very different terms, can be found in the work of Scottish writers during the Thatcher years. Finally, with this background in mind, I deal briefly with the scenario for arts, education and culture being developed by the Cultural Commission before returning to the theme of capital cities in the context of Edinburgh's world recognition through UNESCO.

I

I once lived in Rome, the Ur-capital of the West. (Unless we want to go back to the land of Gilgamesh. Which we have – oops.)

My job took me all over Italy; I travelled where I pleased. The loathing of Rome was universal. Driving through Catania one day, lost in the terrific chaos of its baroque splendor, I was reprimanded by a Carabiniere for executing a daring move. One made in slow motion as it were, in a ballet with the other cars – I assure you it was perfectly safe. On seeing our roman number plates his eyes bulged. 'And you!' he screamed in genuine outrage, 'who think you come from the cradle of *civilisation*!'

The civilisation of capital cities is a bit like that. Taken as a whole it can arouse distinctly ambivalent feelings. For example, we are all familiar with these lofty verses:

> Edina! Scotia's darling seat,
> All hail thy palaces and tow'rs,
> Where once, beneath a Monarch's feet,
> Sat Legislation's sov'reign pow'rs.

But we are all familiar with the philippic of 'A Parcel of Rogues' too.

II

The fact is that our allegiance to capital cities is somewhat schizophrenic. We invest in them politically, legislatively and psycho-socially. As such, they function as analogues for nationhood. In this symbolic way the capital becomes an abstract city, an idea that is flexible enough to aggregate the sum of the nation. It is the stage for a nation's symbolic and ceremonial idea of itself – but here the agreement ends. Because the actual city is real and its space of action is also bitterly contested, challenged and resented. There are other just as powerful symbols to which people can pledge allegiance. Even if the capital is the seat of government, just who do these citizens think they are? Whom do they represent?

At times, then, one might almost be speaking of a foreign city. Both concrete and indeterminate; both of the nation and alienated from it, both of the state and a state within the state – the capital is a kind of Vatican City, a cuckoo in the nest. There is something schizoid about it. And it so happens that Edinburgh demonstrates a particularly strong example of this doubleness in action. Perhaps that is one reason why it gave rise to some of literature's earliest and greatest expressions of multiplicity in Hogg's *Confessions* and Stevenson's *Dr Jekyll and Mr Hyde*.

Our relation to capital cities is therefore far from straightforward. In a political sense, it is from here that the *techne* of governance issues, exerting its force upon the nation throughout history. And the deployment of this *techne* is not necessarily for democratic purposes. But perhaps the history of language is more apposite given the present scenario of Edinburgh as a knowledge city, a city of the word; and here one doesn't have to be Levi-Strauss to understand that for millennia the word was used not as an instrument of enlightenment but of oppression.

Today this is a curious idea, even though we acknowledge the nexus of language and power, and even while we remain reconciled neither to Scots nor Gaelic in any real sense. To which we can add, this also being Britain, the instantly class-conscious relations we have to the accents of our interlocutors. While the deployment of the word and its power in Scotland also has a proud democratic history represented by John Knox's universal parish-based education system, and Edinburgh's reputation as a centre of illumination – to give just two examples – there are nevertheless plenty of skeletons in our cupboard.

III

Every age needs its own stories. But what if, of all the stories we tell, the ones we tell about ourselves are the most untrue?

IV

Let's return to Burns' poem on Edinburgh quoted above. In one sense it is standard eulogistic stuff – Edinburgh is Scotia's 'darling seat', the focus of the nation's aspirations. But, as the verse acknowledges, the sovereignty and legislature is gone. The word 'once' says it all. Self-determination remains, nostalgically – notionally, not actually. Burns' post-1707 hymn has a giant hole in the middle of it. And in this vacuum-like situation other stories develop by way of compensation. These compensatory stories function as surrogates for the missing story of power. Whatever else they speak about, they must carry this freight. The site of conflicting forces, they offer their parables of identity against its negative definition, Burns' 'once'. This makes for powerful narratives, but not entirely reliable history. Pushed by this need to define an identity under threat, they display a tendency to romanticise the past and to exaggerate the cultural homogeneity. The picture of Scotland that emerges from them is only partially authentic. The case of MacPherson's 'Ossian', first passed off as a national epic but in reality a wonderful fake, is particularly fascinating in this regard. Scott provides a similarly good example of this complexity. But while we might question the authenticity of his portrayal of Highland culture, for instance, it is also obvious that in the absence of a legislature, writers like Scott (along with the Kirk and the Law) fulfilled a crucially important role in giving expression to an identifiable political voice *in absentia*, thus ensuring in literature a certain continuity important to the nation. An example of this can be found in the opinions of Mrs Howden, in Scott's *The Heart of Midlothian*. 'I dinna ken muckle about the law,' she says, 'but I ken, when we had a king, and a chancellor, and parliament-men o' our ain, we could aye peeble them wi' stanes if they werena gude bairns – But naebody's nails can reach the length o' Lunnon.'[2]

In this crucial sense, then, writers have functioned through the centuries in Scotland as weather vanes, bearing witness to the drama of the nation. They are not just writers of stories, but commentators upon the vexed issue of national identity. And if this is true of the 1700s and 1800s, it is also true more recently, especially after the debacle of the 1979 devolution referendum. As a response to this political failure, which gave rise once again to a sense of cultural insecurity, many writers returned to the theme of Scottishness in order to reassess and repossess it in an imaginative sense. Perhaps significantly, the expression of this was centred in Glasgow, the city which gained and lost the most from the British Empire. Alasdair Gray's *Lanark* is regarded as the key text in this regard.[3]

This Glasgow-based movement includes the work of writers such as William McIlvanney and James Kelman – and many others. Their work is of course radically different from that of the romantic era mentioned above. But it has nevertheless been characterised as a 'proletarian romanticism', suggesting certain deeper continuities of outlook. All the same, the attitude these writers take to the idea of Scottish identity is significantly different in that the parables they offer no longer attempt to be coherent – or indeed picturesque! The meta-narrative that one might trace in Scott, freighted with ideas of national unity and cultural coherence, now takes on a much more fractured form. The question of identity is now problematised to the extent that it becomes less about the nation than about the individual's state of mind. What Scotland are we talking about when we speak of it? What is the truth of its history? And, more particularly, how does this history relate to me? There is a great difference between thinking of Scotland as a concept and regarding it as a state of mind. The point is neatly captured by Brian McCabe in his novel *The Other McCoy*:

'Scotland is a state of mind,' said McCoy.
'That's very true,' said MacRae . . .
'To Scotland as a concept,' said MacRae.
'No. A state of mind,' corrected Grogan.
'He's right, it's different,' said McCoy.
And they all toasted Scotland as a state of mind.[4]

V

Today, with the opening of the new Parliament, the situation is once again different. Our Mrs Howdens have a target again for their metaphorical stones. But despite the work of the post-1979 generation of writers, that missing story of power, identity and culture mentioned above is still to some extent rattling around in our cupboard. How do we address it?

I have argued that before attempting to script scenarios about our future, we must first script a more complex and contradictory story of our past. This could mean we trace it through the literature it has produced and is producing – as I have tried briefly to do – and through a parallel process of historical research and revision as exemplified by Tom Devine's *Scotland's Empire*.[5] We should enjoy this process, indeed we should revel in the complexities and debates it throws up. It should be no surprise that this project is being led by our historians and writers. One might say that it has always been so. Scotland is a nation built on a particularly strong relation with the word, with its oral power, written sanctity and concrete law.

Three years before the Union of 1707, Andrew Fletcher of Saltoun declared that 'if a man were permitted to make all the ballads, he need not care who should make the laws of a nation' – an opinion now inscribed on the wall of the new Parliament. In this sense Scotland's diverse essence can be recovered and given voice through the multilingual stories of its prose, drama, poetry and oral tradition. This does not mean that we should swallow these stories whole, for we have a responsibility to understand the social conditions under which they were first made and to have a critical relation to them. Naturally, the relationship between literature, power, history and identity has been rich and strong, and not always comfortable. But at its best, as exemplified by James Robertson's novel *Joseph Knight*,[6] these strands can be drawn together in a powerful narrative and linguistic project which brilliantly captures the contradictions, ironies and hard won verities of our history. To read *Joseph Knight* (and indeed *The Fanatic*, Robertson's other historical novel[7]) is to experience a particularly moving and paradoxical *unity*, which, because it embraces complexity, acquires an extraordinary power to resolve the tensions of history.

I want to suggest then that scenarios that will sustain us and move us forward in the future will be those scripted by our historians and writers. But ultimately I believe that fictions are a stronger means than any science because their imaginative power is non-linear and contains, in a Whitmanesque sense, multitudes. In short, we need to develop our imaginative and critical grasp of ourselves in order to have an informed opinion about what our future might be. This might be achieved in a variety of ways. As an example of a contribution to this process, James Robertson became the first ever writer-in-residence at the Scottish Parliament in November 2004 through the Scottish Book Trust. Appropriately enough, in a reprisal of historical and literary memory, he offered MSPs three short courses in the relations between Scottish literature and ideas about power, identity and location. (This essay draws on those courses, though the views expressed are my own.) The results will be published by Scottish Book Trust in early 2005 alongside a newly commissioned work arising out of the experience of the residency itself.[8]

VI

So much then for our own individual 'attitudes of mind'. Meanwhile the government itself has not been idle. The Cultural Commission set up by government has used the language of the scenario to set out its terms. James Boyle, tasked with the business of reorganising the cultural sector, has already spoken of a desire to script the story of what Scotland will be like in 20 years' time. 'What kind of Scotland do we want?' has been his call to all those who have a stake in that cultural question. Equally significantly, the premise assumes that while this is above all a *cultural* question, it is one which encapsulates all areas of the future of the nation, from social justice to economic performance.

At the same time, though based in Edinburgh, he has been careful to set up offices around the country and a process of consultation. The Commission has stated that its prime task in deciding upon these issues is to start from the point of the citizen's 'cultural rights'. However, at the time of writing, it is apparent that there is considerable tension between the Cultural Commission and local government, as expressed through COSLA's (Convention of Scottish Local Authorities) rival commission on the future of the arts. Perhaps one might have expected as much in the relations between central and local government, between the capital and the country.

As the basis for a scenario, the notion of cultural rights is at first sight relatively straightforward. But it is perhaps more complex and contradictory in practice, especially if the end aim is to legislate by 2007. Many might say that rights entail duties. And though one might be able to reduce these to the simple duty of paying tax, the wider notion of what a cultural duty might be is unclear. (Is one, for instance, to beat oneself up for not having read *A Scots Quair*? Perhaps so!) But there is also the sobering thought that cultural rights can only really exist if there is an infrastructure capable of delivering access to them.

The real point here is that the citizen can hardly be expected to exercise rights if it is not clear what they are and what they entail – or indeed what their tangible benefits are. Culture is not obligatory and neither is cultural awareness. The concept of rights must thus be concerned less with creating definitions than with alerting people to the fact that they have an open choice to participate, whether they exercise that right or not. The route to success would therefore seem to be in inculcating a motivation to participate through creating a sense of aspiration, expectation, excitement and creative possibility in an arena where there are visible opportunities for all.

If this is true, the educational sector must be the key area of operation, the arena in which a lifelong engagement with the arts and a set of cultural assumptions and expectations which fuel that engagement can be inculcated and offered to all. Parallel to this must be a similar process applied to the home environment, led by parents who are aspiring for their children for a set of good, easily identifiable and achievable reasons. If we are truly to fulfill the long-term vision outlined, we must start here by redefining our concept of education, understanding it as a 'total' process and not merely a curriculum-based set of engagements. While the curriculum remains the focus for fostering the core tools with which to participate in the culture of society, the wider concept of education can only begin to start here.

But this is not just, or even exclusively, a project about cultural recovery with democratic overtones. It also has to do with creating a truly post-industrial knowledge economy. In other words, even if one does not buy the cultural argument that the arts are beneficial to the individual in itself, one is bound to acknowledge that in today's and tomorrow's economy it is knowledge, technology and ideas that will make us prosper. Investing in creative opportunities for all by imbedding creativity in education is a wise response to the social, economic and cultural challenges that lie ahead – a win/win investment scenario which will carry social, ethical and economic advantage.

VII

Many of the ideas, tensions and themes touched on above regarding literature, the nation, power and location are also relevant to the scripting of a further scenario now being validated and fleshed out: Edinburgh as a City of Literature. James Boyle features again, this time as the chair of the management committee, which after a smartly savvy campaign to UNESCO was rewarded this designation – the first of its kind – in October 2004. The designation comes under a wider programme that has as its objective a worldwide network of creative cities enjoined to share cultural links and stimulate knowledge transfer. The transfer will take place at a literary level, but also – and perhaps more importantly – at the level of educational strategy, resources and access strategies. There are obvious benefits, both economic and cultural. An economic impact study has identified an estimated yearly benefit of £2.2 million for Edinburgh, and a spin-off of £2.1 million for the rest of Scotland. But cash apart, the initiative might, if managed in the right way, also contribute more powerfully to a re-imagining of Scotland which equips it with self-knowledge, skill, creativity and enterprise for the twenty-first century.

In order to be successful in this respect there is one central tension which needs to be resolved, and this has to do with the degree to which this initiative is seen to be a capital thing. Instead, working through national agencies and frameworks, the initiative needs to demonstrate tangible national benefits. At a practical and philosophical level, in the field of action and ideas, it must articulate the message that the civilisation of a modern capital is about *our* civilisation in all its wonderful, diverse and messy disputation. Or else we are back where we started, with a jaundiced eye. Cue the rattling of a few skeletons.

Marc Lambert is Chief Executive Officer of the Scottish Book Trust.

Notes

1   H Henderson, from a letter to the *Scotsman*, 1966.
2   W Scott, *The Heart of Midlothian* (Oxford: Oxford University Press, 1982, originally published 1818).
3   A Gray, *Lanark: a life in four books* (Edinburgh: Canongate Publishing, 1981).
4   B McCabe, *The Other McCoy* (Edinburgh: Mainstream, 1990).
5   TM Devine, *Scotland's Empire 1600–1815* (London: Allen Lane, 2004).
6   J Robertson, *Joseph Knight* (London: Fourth Estate, 2003).
7   J Robertson, *The Fanatic* (London: Fourth Estate, 2001).
8   In the meantime the courses can be downloaded from www.scottishbooktrust.com

15. Scotland after Barnett
Towards fiscal autonomy

Iain McLean

*Most of us do have just one or two topics on which we could die
happily without ever reading another story.*

*Such as: . . . Scotland plc, Gordon and Tony at Granita, tapas
bars, botox, richlists, wheelie bins, lookalikes, Skibo, parking
wardens, the Barnett Formula, the Atkins Diet, Rod Stewart's
bimbos, Gordon Ramsey's manners, the price of doorknobs at
Holyrood, the Tartan Army's ambassadorial value and Jack
Vettriano.*

Keith Aitken, *Scottish Daily Express*, 11 March 2004

Are you listening there in the back? This is not a chapter about Jack
Vettriano. It is a chapter about the Barnett Formula. Stop fidgeting.
You have to understand something. The tap which controls the flow
of UK tax proceeds into Scotland will be turned off soon. I don't
know when, but certainly before 2020. Before it is turned off, there
has to be a mature public debate in Scotland on what should take its
place. Until recently, the Scottish defining narrative of the Barnett
Formula has been that Scotland deserves all it gets and that anyone
who questions that is no better than Edward II. *Scots, wha hae wi
Dewar bled, Scots, wham Jack has aften led.* . . . But the plucky Scots are
threatened by the demon English who are imposing a wicked Barnett
Squeeze on them. In England, the defining narrative reverses the
roles. The Scots are a bunch of mean and arrogant whingers,

featherbedded by the Barnett Formula that allows them to sup turtle soup with gold spoons while the English have to beg for a crust in the streets of Newcastle.

Things are at last getting a bit more grown-up, with all the Opposition parties, and some leading economists, saying they want fiscal autonomy (sometimes *full fiscal autonomy*). But they mean utterly different things. Some of them are more plausible than others. Once you understand (yes, you at the back) what full fiscal autonomy would involve, you might prefer something quite different, such as a Grants Commission to distribute funds to the four countries (or the 12 regions) of the United Kingdom. Get your jotters out. We are going to talk about four things. *Why Barnett was invented. How it works. Why it can't last. What should replace it.*

Why Barnett was invented

Scotland has enjoyed higher public spending per head than England since about 1900. For that there has been one big reason, and it is not the one that people think. People think that Scotland gets more because it is colder, poorer and has more difficult geography than England. All of these things are true (although 100 years ago and now, it was not much poorer than England). But the reason for higher spending is that *Scotland poses a credible threat to the United Kingdom*. In the 1880s, when formula funding started, it was named the *Goschen proportion* after the Chancellor of the Exchequer in Lord Salisbury's Unionist government. The big problem then was Ireland, not Scotland. To try (vainly in the end) to keep Ireland in the Union, the Unionists threw money at it. This was called *Killing Home Rule by kindness*. Not many people in Scotland wanted to secede, and almost none of them were violent. But governments decided to placate them too, starting with the crofters of Skye, who got the Crofters' Commission (1886 and still with us) to settle their land grievances and prevent them festering as in Ireland.

The Goschen proportion was just 11:80. For every £80 of public spending in England and Wales on programmes it covered, Scotland would get £11, to be spent by the already-devolved Scottish administration under the Secretary (of State) for Scotland. Scotland dropped below 11/80 of the population of England and Wales by 1901, and has continued to drop further below. By the time the ghost of Goschen finally vanished in the 1970s, public spending per head in Scotland was about 20 per cent above that in England (and substantially higher than in Wales, which was as poor and almost as sparsely populated as Scotland, although it has fewer midges). The secretary of state could protect the Goschen proportion because he had a credible threat at his back. He could tell the Cabinet that unless they protected Scotland's spending share the Nationalists would start winning elections, and where would the United Kingdom be then? All secretaries of state have done this, but the supreme practitioners have been Tom Johnston (Lab., 1941–5), Willie Ross (Lab., 1964–70 and 1974–6), Ian Lang (Cons., 1990–5) and Michael Forsyth (Cons., 1995–7). It is easier for Conservatives, because theirs after all is the Conservative *and Unionist* Party. Although public spending in England was squeezed during the Thatcher administrations, the gap with Scotland stayed as wide as ever.

In summer 1974, Prime Minister Harold Wilson overruled Willie Ross and Labour's Scottish executive, and announced that the party favoured devolution. This was to head off the expected SNP triumph in the polls. In fact, the electoral system did for them more effectively than Wilson. In October 1974, the SNP got 30 per cent of the vote to the Conservatives' 24 per cent, but only 11 seats to the Conservatives' 16. Labour retained the majority of Scottish seats on a minority vote. Nevertheless it had been a very close shave. On 35 per cent of the vote, the SNP would have swept the board, won more than half the seats in Scotland, and started to negotiate independence. Therefore, Labour prepared its flagship devolution plans. The Treasury started to prepare for life after devolution, and conducted (some would say bullied the Scottish and Welsh Offices into) a Needs Assessment. This assessment, not published until 1979, gave the following numbers for the relative needs and the actual spending in the four countries of the UK, for the services that the Scotland and Wales Acts would have devolved (see table 1).

Table 1   HM Treasury 'Needs Assessment', 1979 (data for 1976–7).

	England	Scotland	Wales	Northern Ireland
Relative needs assessment	100	116	109	131
Actual spending levels 1976–7	100	122	106	135

Source: HM Treasury *Needs Assessment – Report* (1979), esp. para. 6.5

But by 1979, devolution was dead. An English backlash caused a government defeat which killed the original flagship bill in 1977. Separate bills for Scotland and Wales were then enacted, but the rebels added sections requiring a referendum on the plans, with a 'Yes' vote not to be confirmed unless at least 40 per cent of the electorate voted Yes. In Wales, the referendum led to a crushing No; in Scotland to a faint Yes, far below the 40 per cent threshold. The government fell on a Conservative–SNP confidence vote, and the reign of Mrs Thatcher began.

However, the Treasury's other preparative step has lasted. This was the Barnett Formula, so named (by David Heald in 1980) after Joel Barnett, the Chief Secretary to the Treasury from 1974 to 1979. Barnett's officials designed the Formula as a temporary expedient to reduce Scotland's relative spending advantage until a needs-based formula could be introduced. Lord Barnett, as he now is, told a Commons select committee that he expected 'his' formula would not last more than 'a year or even 20 minutes'.[1] It has not only lasted, but was embedded into the 1997 devolution settlement. The white papers outlining the Labour government's plans for Scotland and Wales announced that the Barnett arrangements for funding their spending blocks would continue. Although not announced, this policy also applied to Northern Ireland. However, the Formula is not statutory. It is not in the Scotland or Wales Acts, and it could be revoked unilaterally by a future UK government. Lord Barnett used to be proud of the fame his formula had brought him, but he now dislikes its unfairness so much that he would like to remove his name from it.

How it works

Some of you may want to understand the differential equation system for the Barnett Formula. You will have to stay on after class. For the rest of you, here is what you need to know. The Barnett Formula is not about needs. It is just based on relative population. It leaves unchanged the baseline block grant from year to year. It merely stipulates that for every £1 of *extra* spending in England each year, Scotland (and Wales and Northern Ireland) will get an increase in their block grant proportionate to their relative populations. Originally the proportions were set arbitrarily at 85:10:5 for England, Scotland and Wales. So, for every 85p of extra spending in England, Scotland would get 10p added to its block grant, and Wales 5p. These population proportions were too generous to Scotland (and too mean to Wales) until altered by that hammer of the Scots Michael Portillo in 1992 to the correct population proportions. Now they are rebased after every spending review for the next two years. So they track Scotland's (declining) share of the British population, but with a time-lag that works in Scotland's favour.

Without doing the maths, the property of this formula is that in the long run it will converge until spending per head is the same in all four countries of the UK. In the long run, the original 1979 baseline, under which each country got more per head than England, becomes swamped by the successive increments added every year, until spending per head is imperceptibly different from identical in all four countries.

The long run has been longer than anyone anticipated in 1978. Up to 1999 there was no perceptible convergence, even though the Barnett Formula supposedly operated throughout. Elsewhere we have given some technical reasons for this,[2] but the main one is political. For all but the last two years of that period, the Conservatives were in office. As the pre-eminently unionist party, they so feared a nationalist threat to the continuation of the United Kingdom that whenever Barnett threatened to produce embarrassing results they bypassed it and found a way to supply off-Barnett goodies to Scotland. The change of government in 1997 caused no immediate change because of Chancellor Brown's hair-shirted decision not to increase the Conservatives' planned spending totals. If there is no increase in England, there is nothing for Barnett to bite on.

So Barnett began to bite only when the Labour government started to increase public spending in England. This grew most in the spending reviews of 2000 and 2002, and less but still substantially in the spending review of 2004. The three territories (as the Treasury calls them) are getting their population share of the extra largesse. But, as a proportion of the baseline that they were getting before, the extra is less than in England. Barnett convergence (in Scotland known as the 'Barnett squeeze') is in progress.

Why it can't last

First the low political reasons, then the principled reasons of public finance. Barnett cannot last because it has no friends outside Scotland. Also it is a lousy formula.

When Treasury officials are asked about the future of Barnett, they have two stock replies. One is 'Nothing is set in stone, but ministers have no plans to alter the Barnett Formula.' The other is 'Ministers have no plans to alter the Barnett Formula, but nothing is set in stone.' I predict that the second reply will shortly crowd out the first. John Prescott, deputy prime minister in the 1997 and 2001 Labour governments, lets his irritation with Barnett break out from time to time. In 2001 he predicted 'blood on the carpet', although the only blood to hit it was Prescott's when he was slapped down by the Prime Minister's press spokesman Alastair Campbell the following day. In March 2004 Prescott told the Newcastle *Journal*, the leading anti-Barnett campaigning newspaper, 'I wouldn't anticipate early changes but the case for reconsidering the basis of funding is getting stronger all the time.'[3] The English regions, especially but not only the poorer ones, hate Barnett because they think it embeds privilege for Scotland. The campaign is strongest in the North East, engine-room of the 1977 defeat of the Scotland and Wales Bill. It is only too obvious there that spending per scholar is much higher in Duns than in Alnwick, and spending per patient is much higher in Berwickshire than in Berwick-on-Tweed. Strictly speaking this difference is not only due to the Barnett Formula but also to the formulae for distributing public expenditure around the regions of England – also broken. But English politicians will continue to put the blame on Barnett. True, English elected assemblies are dead in the water since the defeat of that idea in the North East in November 2004. But the regional lobbies, most powerfully in London, will continue. Nobody who wants to be Mayor of London can fail to campaign against Barnett. If you enter the phrase 'iniquitous Barnett Formula' into the Lexis–Nexis search engine of all British press stories since the late 1980s, you get 24 hits, of which 21 come from the *Journal* (Newcastle upon Tyne), and one each from the *Guardian*, *Daily Telegraph* and *Northern Echo* (Darlington).

More important still, Wales and Northern Ireland have changed sides. If the Needs Assessment (table 1) was right, Barnett never did Wales any favours. As her baseline spending was below her needs, the Barnett squeeze would take Welsh spending further and further below needs. Instead of converging towards relative need, it would diverge away from it. Under the Conservatives, this was masked by the generosity of the Unionist secretaries of state. Under Labour, the quiescence of Welsh Labour is more puzzling. It may be because their eyes were mistakenly fixed on the tawdry prize of EU Objective One status, which will be a broken toy by 2006. Objective One areas are the poorest areas in the European Union. An artificial confection called West Wales and the Valleys has Objective One status. But with ten new member states, all poor, in 2004, no area in the UK will qualify for Objective One in future grant rounds. More likely, Welsh Labour did not want to embarrass UK Labour by criticising it ahead of National Assembly elections. With the poor performance of Plaid Cymru in 2003, that constraint has gone. Expect Welsh Labour to voice its constituents' true interest, which is to scrap Barnett.

Northern Ireland has no elected government at the time of writing, but its civil servants have become anti-Barnett militants. They argue that (even leaving aside security, which mostly does not come under Barnett) Northern Ireland has high spending needs because of its young population, with more children and more of them staying on (in two separate school systems, it has to be added). They believe that by 2006, the block available under Barnett will be insufficient to fund Northern Ireland's needs. It seems that the 1979 needs numbers are still being quietly updated in a Stormont basement.

Academic commentators insist that the formula is a very poor way of distributing block grant. Unless Scotland becomes independent, there will always be a distribution of block grant to Scotland from the UK government. But the Barnett arrangement breaks every rule in the public finance economist's book. It is bad for the UK and bad for Scotland. It is bad for the UK because it distributes grant in a way unrelated to need. It fails to give the UK government control over things it should control and gives it control over things it should not. The UK government remains responsible for macroeconomic management, as the top tier must in any federation. The Chancellor's fiscal rules (the Golden Rule and the Sustainable Investment Rule) are currently the main tools of macro management in government hands. They control the amount of public sector debt and borrowing in the UK. But the UK government cannot control what the devolved administrations do – under the devolution settlement they can switch their block grant between current and capital spending at will.

On the other side, consider higher education, which is a devolved function. In 2003, the UK government produced a large and politically controversial bill to change the financing of higher education in England. The bill, now enacted, had complex knock-on consequences for higher education in Scotland, Wales and Northern Ireland. But when I dug into this a little way, I could find no evidence that UK ministers discussed the proposals' implications with their devolved counterparts.[4] The act channels a large increase in funds to English higher education. Part of this will go through the English education department, and therefore attract a 'Barnett consequential' for the other three countries. But part will go through the research councils, which are on the vote of the Department of Trade and Industry, an all-UK department, and hence attracts no Barnett consequential.

More profoundly, the Barnett arrangements give no incentives for efficiency. Wales and Northern Ireland have no power to tax at all. Scotland has only the 3p in the pound Scottish variable rate of income tax, so far not used. As the Scottish Executive cannot control the amount of money it gets, it might as well just spend it all. Faced with a choice between spending that will make the Scots richer and spending that will not, it has no incentive to choose the former, because it will not see any of the enhanced tax revenue that will result. For that reason, the recent discussions of fiscal autonomy for Scotland are welcome.

What should replace it

Fiscal autonomy comes in two main shades, a nationalist version promoted by SNP politicians, and a devolutionist version promoted by some Conservatives, some Liberal Democrats and some academics.

The nationalist version is just Scottish independence. If the Scots vote for independence in 2007 or later, they should have it. But they should not have illusions about it. Some ingenious sums due to Alex Salmond MP purport to show that Scotland subsidises England. They rest on very dodgy foundations. In particular they assume that almost all North Sea oil revenues would flow to an independent Scotland, and that they would stay robust. But they would not all flow to Scotland; they fluctuate wildly (between £1 billion and £5 billion per annum in the last decade) and they are in long-term decline.

Scotland's true fiscal position is published every year in *Government Expenditure and Revenue in Scotland*, published by the Executive and known to its friends as GERS. Table 2 shows the latest available picture, for financial year 2001/02.

Table 2 shows that an independent Scotland would begin life with a seriously imbalanced budget. It could not sustain public expenditure £8 billion ahead of tax revenue. If oil revenue stayed at its

Table 2 Net borrowing, 2001/02 (excluding North Sea revenues)

	UK, £ million	Scotland, £ million	Share of UK
Aggregate expenditure	390,731	39,428	10.1%
Aggregate receipts	384,825	31,360	8.2%
Net borrowing (NB)	5,906	8,060	
NB as a percentage of GDP	0.6%	10.3%	

Source: Scottish Executive, *Government Expenditure and Revenue in Scotland*, Dec 2003, Table 8.1, at www.scotland.gov.uk/library5/government/gers04-10.asp

2001/02 peak of £5.2 billion and if an independent Scotland got 70 per cent of that, the fiscal gap would close, but only to £4.4 billion. To put this sum into perspective, the Treasury estimates that a 1p change in the Scottish variable rate of income tax in 2002/03 could be worth approximately plus or minus £230 million. The entire 3p in the pound would therefore yield about £700 million – a trivial contribution to closing the fiscal gap.

I am all for Scotland having full fiscal independence. But the Scots should choose it in full awareness of what it would involve.

Turning to the Conservative version of fiscal autonomy, I will describe it in words that they would not necessarily use. Nor do you have to be a Conservative to support it. The Scottish Liberal Democrat conference backed it, against their leaders' advice, and some Labour figures such as Wendy Alexander have started to raise the flag cautiously for what she calls fiscal federalism.[5] The UK has one of the largest *vertical fiscal gaps* (also known as vertical fiscal imbalances – VFI) in the democratic world. A vertical fiscal gap exists when one tier of government has the power to raise tax and another has the duty (or the pleasure) to spend it. The Scottish Executive has the power to vary the standard rate of income tax by up to 3p in the pound. Table 2 shows how trivial this power to tax is, in comparison with the gap between government revenue and government expenditure in Scotland. The Welsh and Northern Irish assemblies have no power to tax, and none is proposed for English regional assemblies either. Local government, which in the three territories is funded from their Barnett blocks, in England is funded by another set of broken formulae. Here again VFI is unusually high by international standards. Local government spends about 25 per cent of the identifiable public spending in England, but raises only about 4 per cent of the tax receipts because it has access to only one tax base, namely domestic real estate, taxed via the regressive and unsatisfactory council tax.

VFI is a bad thing. It reduces the incentives for central and local government to tax efficiently, and it encourages politicians to play games against one another. Especially, to play blame games. If citizens are unclear who provides which service then each tier of government can blame the other. As Scotland is not fiscally autonomous, Scots politicians can turn from the difficult task of providing good public services to the easier task of blaming their problems on the English. That is admittedly harder for Labour than for the Opposition. But the Executive's displacement activities from fiscal reality rationally take the form of defending Barnett when it has no other friends in the world. When it disappears, as it must, they will face a tougher world. If the Scottish Executive raised more of what it spent, say the fiscal autonomists, it would face the tougher world immediately, to maybe short-term pain but long-term gain. Scots politicians and Scots citizens would face the true costs and the true trade-offs between public services and tax savings. Fiscal autonomy would require radical change. We have listed elsewhere,[6] in an English local government context, the tax changes that would be needed. For Scotland, Wales and Northern Ireland they would be similar:

○ First, the three devolved authorities must each have the same power to tax. If it was right for Labour to argue in 1997 that the Scottish Executive should have the power to tax (and I believe that it was), then the power should have been given to Wales and Northern Ireland as well.

- ○ Second, the UK must 'vacate some tax points' (in Canadian terminology) – that is, allow a certain proportion of, say, VAT and income tax receipts to be kept by the devolved administrations.
- ○ Third, the taxation of real estate must become more progressive and more comprehensive. That old Liberal favourite, a land value tax, is the best way. We argued that it would take time to introduce,[7] but that the target for introducing it should be 2009, the centenary year of Lloyd George's People's Budget, of which land taxation was intended to be the culmination.

This regime would introduce *fiscal federalism* to the UK. Fiscal federalism is familiar to Americans, Canadians and Australians, but as yet little understood in the UK. A recent pamphlet for the Fraser of Allander Institute[8] gives fuller details than space permits here. I have also published brief studies of the Canadian and Australian systems, which will be revised and republished in 2005 in a book called *The Fiscal Crisis of the UK*.[9] Fiscal federalism reduces VFI by making each tier of government responsible for raising what it spends – or at least a higher proportion of what it spends. The Scottish variable rate of income tax would not be serious fiscal federalism even if implemented, because it could only fund a laughably trivial proportion of Scottish public expenditure. Serious fiscal federalism requires the Scottish Executive to raise a serious amount of tax revenue, and/or requires the UK government to assign a serious proportion of its tax revenue to Scotland (and Wales and Northern Ireland). At the end of their excellent discussion of versions of fiscal federalism for Scotland, MacDonald and Hallwood reject the more ambitious versions of fiscal autonomy for good economic reasons, and call for a system that:

- ○ extends the assignment of revenues from an agreed range of taxes and the devolution of a further range of taxes
- ○ preserves a significant equalisation grant to ensure equity

considerations are not sacrificed unduly, in line with good practice across the globe

o   provides for an agreed regional borrowing capacity.[10]

If the emperor of fiscal autonomy, once stripped of any comfort blankets, is naked, then the other viable alternative to Barnett is a needs assessment regime. But 'needs' are what philosophers call an essentially contested concept. Every location in the UK would claim that what it happened to lack, it needed. Where needs formulae already exist, in local government and health funding, we see the results of decades of lobbying embedded in the needs formulae. For instance, the Scottish local government needs formula includes a weighting for miles of road built on peat. The English school needs formula includes a weighting for ethnic minority pupils. If you have a lot of roads built on peat and a lot of ethnic minority pupils, you can readily see why you need more public spending per head. If you do not, you may not.

A future territorial needs formula must be the engine of MacDonald and Hallwood's 'significant equalisation grant to ensure equity'. It must ensure that each comparable citizen of the UK is treated equally wherever he or she lives; and it must be compatible with economic efficiency. The second criterion requires that there be no incentives to politicians to make their territory appear 'needy' – something for which the present English regime (and, it must be said, the present EU regime) is notorious. In several recent publication we have proposed a regime that meets these criteria.[11] There would be a Territorial Grants Commission, modelled on the highly successful Commonwealth Grants Commission of Australia. It would be an arms-length body like the Electoral Commission or the Committee on Standards in Public Life – appointed by politicians, but thereafter unable to be intimidated by them. Its commissioners would be appointed by agreement between the UK government and all the territorial governments, including those of London and any other self-governing English regions. Its staff would be public servants drawn or seconded from the relevant agencies such as the devolved administrations, the Treasury, the Office for National Statistics, and the Office of the Deputy Prime Minister. Each territory with an elected government would have one vote at meetings, and there would be a mechanism for ensuring that those English regions without elected assemblies also got votes.

There would be two mutually dependent ground rules. The first is that decisions on block grant must be taken unanimously. This is to give each region the same bargaining power, and avoid regions threatening to cause trouble if they do not get their way. But, as a unanimity rule on its own could easily produce deadlock, the second ground rule is that if agreement is not reached by the known deadline for decision, then the additional grant to each territory for the following year will be inversely proportional to the GDP of that territory. This 'inverse GDP rule' is both fairer and more efficient than Barnett. It would lead in the long run not to equal spending per head, which cannot be the right target, but to spending proportional to the need of each region. But regions would not have an incentive to be, or remain, poor. As public spending per head is less than GDP per head, it follows that a regional government which raises its region's GDP per head will always gain more from that than it would lose in public spending under the inverse GDP rule.

Scotland in 2020 will be more fiscally autonomous than it is now. That may have its painful side. But it should produce a self-confident, fiscally mature country, not the nation of spongers and whingers that is sometimes portrayed in the southern media. A country I would be proud to retire to.

Iain McLean is Professor of Politics at Oxford University and a Fellow of Nuffield College. He is author of The Legend of Red Clydeside *and numerous papers and studies on devolution, finance and representation.*

Notes

1   House of Commons Treasury Committee, *Second Report: the Barnett Formula*, HC 341 (London: TSO, 1997), p 1.

2   I McLean and A McMillan, 'The distribution of public expenditure across the UK regions', *Fiscal Studies* 24 (2003): 45–71.

3   Interview with John Prescott, *Journal* (Newcastle upon Tyne), 3 March 2004.

4   I McLean, 'Devolution bites', *Prospect*, March 2003.

5   W Alexander, 'It's time to look beyond independence', *Scotsman*, 22 Sept 2004.

6   I McLean and A McMillan, *New Localism, New Finance* (London: New Local Government Network, 2003).

7   McLean and McMillan, *New Localism, New Finance*.

8   R MacDonald and P Hallwood, *The Economic Case for Fiscal Federalism in Scotland*, The Allander Series (Glasgow: Fraser of Allander Institute, 2004).

9   I McLean, 'Fiscal federalism in Canada', Nuffield College Working Papers on Politics, no 2003-W17, 2003 (available at www.nuff.ox.ac.uk/Politics/papers/); I McLean, 'Fiscal federalism in Australia', *Public Administration* 82 no 1 (2004): 21–38; I McLean, *The Fiscal Crisis of the United Kingdom* (Basingstoke: Palgrave, 2005).

10   MacDonald and Hallwood, *The Economic Case for Fiscal Federalism in Scotland*, p 55.

11   McLean and McMillan, 'The distribution of public expenditure across the UK regions'; McLean and McMillan, *New Localism, New Finance*.

16. Scotland, Europe and the World Crisis

Regionalism and Scotland's shifting position between Britain and Europe

Christopher Harvie

Regionalism revisited

Two events of the first week of November 2004, vastly different in scale – the reinstatement of George Bush in the White House, and the collapse of New Labour's plans for English devolution – may have a revolutionary impact on Scottish politics. The link was dramatised by the Black Watch in Iraq, but waters seem to be warming under the ice which has for a decade frozen Anglo–Scottish relationships.

At one level these are to do with the frustrations of European unification, and consequently involve tendencies within late capitalism. At another they stem from the peculiar nature of British centralism. The fashionable gurus of metropolitan society have found a ready audience for disparagements of regionalism, as in this outpouring from Ralf Dahrendorf:

> *A new regionalism is rapidly gaining ground at the end of the twentieth century, and it is tribal in character. People look for homogeneous units, and thereby turn their backs on the larger heterogeneous nation-states which the nineteenth century created. Sometimes they claim that their Catalonia, Slovakia or Wallonia will connect more easily with the globalised network of a new age; but the probability must be high that these allegedly homogeneous regions will in fact resemble Chechnya or Bosnia*

> *or other war-torn areas. Intolerance within and aggressiveness*
> *without are a frequent concomitant of nationalism.*[1]

Such emoting seemed to run directly against the argument in my *Rise of Regional Europe*,[2] that with the shift of 'high politics' from national capitals to Brussels and Strasbourg, social and economic initiatives would almost automatically make a practical and profitable move to smaller regional or cultural–national identities, highly technologised, environmentally aware, steered by representatives of Lord Dahrendorf's *Bildungsburgertum*. Had Dahrendorf seen *Braveheart*? His response was logically strange but by no means unique. A German ought to be the last to praise 'large' nation-statehood. Wallonia and Catalonia (urban-industrial, though in their time victims of 'large nation-state' fascism) cannot be classed with Bosnia and Chechnya (ex-communist peasantry on the Muslim– Christian divide). Dahrendorf, who has been keeping some strange right-wing neoliberal company lately, has been echoed on the London–New York beat by well-heeled tellymen like Simon Schama and Niall Ferguson. The mantra that centralisation is *ipso facto* good hovers about in the same media who accept a unipolar America-steered world – hear the whoops of joy coming from *The Times* on the North East poll – putting the little platoons again on the defensive.

The Rise of Regional Europe stemmed from scripting 'grasping the thistle' for the BBC's *Scotland 2000* series in 1986/87, which helped start the autonomy drive. My line was roughly as above, and for the last quarter-century I have lived a regionalist life, between Scotland, Baden-Württemberg and Wales (and in the course of daily life, between Ba-Wü, France and Belgium across now-insignificant frontiers) with few crises, even in 1989–91: a Scotsman free in Europe, if you like, achieving at least personally what in 1986 Jim Sillars had argued for the country as a whole.

In *Scotland: the case for optimism*,[3] Sillars reckoned that we could thus slip many of our British moorings without awakening the traumas of DIVORCE, and that our prime alignment seemed to be with the European core and in particular with the bourgeois regions –

roughly the representatives of 'Rhenish welfare-capitalism' – which were renewing technical and social structures in a sustainable way, while blurring the frontiers between traditional nation states. Compare Strasbourg and Freiburg with British towns like Bristol and Southampton or, alas, with anywhere in Scotland. QED.

But during my Tübingen stint the imponderables multiplied – not least Sillars himself – and now we have to look at continental developments through the war-shattered prism of a pillaged former Comecon (Council for Mutual Economic Assistance), Euro–American diplomatic breakdown and an Anglo–American addiction to big stick politics. True, Scotland and Wales got partial autonomy, and Northern Ireland got a very complex 'un-settlement', in 1997/98, but were these real concessions by a traditionally overmighty centralist state or 'buying off trouble' while any sort of symmetrical federalism vanished into the distance? They accompanied the blotting out of non-London from the metropolitan media and, perhaps, a tendency for Downing Street to bash the spirit-stirring war-drum when crises loomed within devolved politics. More ominously, European reaction to Balkan instability and the slapdash interventions of Anglo–America seemed to be the rise of something akin to Dahrendorf's bogey: a regional conservatism, living off economic downturn and anti-refugee emotions, and shifting governments of the centre-right – notably in Austria and Italy – to the right-right?

One full term of the Scottish Parliament has also been a sobering experience. No more a failure than Westminster or good ol' Bagehotian Cabinet government – Jack McConnell actually attends it daily – it has shown the difficulties of operating with existing party, industrial, administrative and media structures. It has faced cumulative socioeconomic and running-in problems which have reduced our Scots Whitehall to division if not impotence, and the economic parallels with German *Länder* which seemed to work in 1986 look less convincing today. Scots MPs have not moved north in droves, as both Neal Ascherson and James Naughtie had expected in 1986, and waning party membership (under 1.2 per cent of the electorate compared with about 5 per cent in Germany) has damaged the list MSP system. An emigré élite – from Blair, Cook to Lord Robertson of NATO and Rupert Murdoch of the Powers of Darkness – has continued, and while the profile of Scots Westminster MPs *as individuals* is subterranean, they remain an important sinister interest enabling Blair to rule against his own party.

The present multiple crises make it difficult (though necessary) to analyse where Europe is going and how it fits world politics, where British development relates (or doesn't relate) to it and where Scotland features in this.

After the wall

The story is that Europe changed profoundly in 2004. The EU now has 25 nation states, many smaller and poorer than Scotland, and has seemingly drifted far from the possible Europe of the regions of 1988–92, and possibly from the Treaty of Rome ethos. Perhaps the result comes closer to the Locarno pact of the inter-war years: an alliance with the small democracies which are the buffer-zone between it: a West European 'core' (with or without Britain) and an ever-problematic Russia.

Is the re-emergence of core Europe a bad thing? Unipolarity seemed part of the inevitabilism of the likes of Fukuyama, Dahrendorf, etc in 1991, but has it worked in practice? The world is a lot more dangerous than in the Carter–Brezhnev era when the USSR was always the 'alternative' which could be appealed to by those frustrated by the Americans, and in return the Russians could patch things up within the context of balance-of-power relationships. The Americans were circumspect and the dull old men in the Kremlin mollified the Russians. Frustration with the One Super-power has developed its own nihilistic responses, seemingly impervious to mediation, and the USSR has collapsed into criminality and police-state rule. The eyes of the Americans and the Russians have become fixed on that territory around the Caucasus which the long-dead founder of geopolitics, Sir Halford MacKinder, *quondam* Unionist MP for Maryhill, saw as the Heartland of the

World Island, where oil, drugs and Muslim fundamentalism bubble threateningly away.

Gorbachev and the (few) articulate reformers of 1985–91 had their eyes fixed on the European social market, not on neoliberalism. Eastern central planning was doomed after Chernobyl and the oil price fall, but this took with it, as well as Comecon centralism, a huge black economy which involved German Ossi factories manufacturing for Wessi concerns and Ossi municipalities burying Wessi rubbish: a low-wage input into a high-tech economy, ignored by nearly all the liberal accounts – Dahrendorf, Garton Ash, etc – of reunification. If the Bundesrepublik Deutschland (BRD) stalled after reconstruction, about 1995, this really was what was wrong with it. The ground has mostly been made up in the Rhenish regions: the population of Baden-Württemberg may be up 10 per cent over the decade with ex-Ossis and *Spataussiedlers* from Russia, but there's been little social discord. Biotech has flourished, along with computerised engineering and environmental engineering, the Mercedes 'A-class' and the 'Smart', the Karlsruhe supertrams and ICE (InterCityExpress) trains doing their stuff for not-so-traditional metal-bashing. Housing as a social service has coped with the population expansion – though speculation in it has not been there to trigger a high street boom and, anyway, the Germans react to a downturn by saving. When Britain's 'incapacitated' (three times the German level) are counted in, unemployment is no worse. But the post-unification hiatus has worked to the advantage of the 'Anglo-Saxons'.

Will there be an evolutionary or revolutionary outcome to this competition between systems? A reversion towards a regionalised 'core' Europe with strong democratic institutions and civil society, deployed against American globalisation? Or something more fraught? Dahrendorf's panic provides one indicator, but ethnic nationalism isn't the only predator. The notion that global US capitalism is benign, and that regionalism could piggy-back on it, looks very remote after Enron and WorldCom.

But if globalism has called time on Britain, what future for Scotland or Wales? Was the restoration of our 'covenanted sovereignty' an antiquarian enterprise in a post-modern world? Do we face a populist xenophobia, divorced from actual power, but all the more potent for *not* engaging with verifiable data for economic success: *Braveheart* and the Serbian way? There are, as any urban Saturday will demonstrate, enough sour old grievances powered by underemployed, drunk young men to fuel this.

The question of 'Iron Broon'

After America voted, there was stunned silence overall, but the most intriguing inaudibility came from Gordon Brown, who might be expected to benefit from Blair's embarrassment. The failure of the arch-Anglo-Saxonist Brown to promote reindustrialisation has been the more salient as he has been, in the absence of proto-federal institutions, the determiner of Scottish politics who in 1999 celebratedly 'took a baseball bat to the SNP'.

In the 1970s *Red Paper* Brown had supported a 'dynamic region' role for Scotland.[4] And indeed, within the EU the record of the smaller western members had been pretty good, compared with the UK: 35 per cent richer, enjoying 64 per cent faster growth, smaller deficits and lower unemployment – and this was to leave out post-1986 'Celtic Tiger' Ireland. But both Brown's and Sillars's arguments were overtaken by events. What use now are the Common Agricultural and Fisheries policies and the Regional Fund to Scotland? Sillars wanted Scotland to play like Ireland, combining participation in Council of Ministers and Commission with playing the Brussels game in the national interest. But in 1986, when he published, the Irish economy started to surge forward, going in 12 years from under 60 per cent of British GDP to near parity. It's unlikely that this – driven by a favourable demography, shrewd choice of technological options (pharmaceuticals and software) and huge if generally under-regarded direct American investment – will recur.

The Thatcher–Major years saw the plundering of the public sector, a 'victimless crime' concealed by rising share values. Brown failed to remedy this, and in the absence of any coherent forward planning – for the Monetary Policy Committee of the Bank has little industrial input and no regional remit – the Scottish situation has become infective. Leading sectors – the Post Office, power generation, the railways, the NHS – are beset by constant upheaval and these have now become as typical of Britain as high-street-led economic growth, a burgeoning trade deficit, a pensions industry imperilled by stock-market decline and unsustainable household debt. The *quality* of such economic growth is, unsurprisingly, being queried by the likes of Professor Andrew Oswald who argued in 2004 that real improvement in living standards, measured by the actual happiness of society, has not happened since the 1950s.[5]

Judged against such experience, 'Old Europe' has done better than Britain infrastructurally, industrially and socially. Baden-Württemberg and Germany have since 1989 coped with population increase and fearsome environmental problems with little political upheaval or growth in support for the far right. On the wider map this period has seen political tendencies which have (with the end of the Cold War and the 'renationalisation' of fiscal policy in the run-up to the Euro) frustrated and deflected regionalism. The destabilisation of the Balkans and the accompanying refugee crisis has also boosted right-wingers (on closer examination more racist than regional) – from Haider's FPÖ in Austria to the Sill-Partei in Hamburg – yet few of these have sustained themselves.

Our plutonic economy?

The challenge to the small states within and around Old Europe is in the long term to re-balance the situation by increasing their socio-economic synergy: using the technological competencies of the EU and the advanced regions but developing their social and cultural resources to act as a counter to multinational and American hegemons. Old Europe has been circumspect, not unenterprising. In civic terms a society which recycles 50 per cent of its rubbish, repairs footwear and electrical goods instead of junking them, walks and cycles or goes by bus and train inevitably registers less in the growth stakes than one which shops its head off, fly-tips its waste and drives everywhere. This synergy can promote what Jeremy Rifkin call the 'third sector' of *spieltrieb* (using the motives of affection, enthusiasm, local loyalty) to regenerate our economy as well as our civil society.

But there is also Rifkin's 'fourth sector', in *The Age of Access*,[6] of great and unalterable equality, archaic great power nationalism, plus the black economy plus crime. This has been rapidly gaining on us, in a combination of 'white van man'-type enterprise: the subject of Hans-Magnus Enzensberger's morose essay 'The Italianisation of Europe',[7] outright criminality, the erosion of the state's monopoly of violence, and 'top-down' corruption through the sheer wealth of individuals unparticular about where their money is coming from. This consolidated type of illegality undermines civil society, while the British political élite's involvement with high-level rule-bending – whether in corporate law or consultancy – inhibits it from intervention. The European record seems little better, with Brussels' centralisation making matters less transparent. The Eurostat scandal, ineptly handled by Neil Kinnock, suggests a quite deliberate attempt to wreck the statistics whose use for comparison ought to be the motor of reform.

If the smaller European states and the regions remain isolated, can we expect more of this? The microstates were economically insignificant until the 1960s and unknown to theory until Tom Nairn's study,[8] in which he identified them – Andorra, Monaco, and a rich variety of British possessions, from the Channel Islands to the Cayman Islands. These were, in Nairn's analysis, the ball-bearings on which international capitalism rolled, maintaining links between its unpresentable element and the huge rewards of its bosses. The record of British banking in money-laundering, etc, is a very dubious one. And of course businesses which are out to expand – by quite legitimate means – smoking, drinking, gambling and pornography have knock-on effects on public expenditure. Providing high-cost remedies in health and education increases the returns to PFI (Private Finance Initiative) concerns.

Moreover the Scoto–British constitutional settlement is unstable. The use of Scottish MPs to support unpopular government policies, plus internal dissidence, has made for party *egoismo*, bureaucratisation and policy stasis, and unchecked centralisation. When the new media regulator – Ofcom – has as minimal a regional input as Gordon Brown's Financial Policy Committee, can anyone regard notions of regional devolution as plausible? Or treat seriously a Scottish 'bonfire of the quangos' which ended up with them bigger than ever, and 70 per cent of their members Labour trusties?

By contrast, the 'Rhenish' regions are still a sober model, and as Old Europe grows together, this internal regionalism will gain, though the Committee of the Regions has, alas, stayed at the talking shop level. In France since the Mitterand reforms of 1981, regional power has been growing towards that exercised by the smaller nation-states. A more effective intermediate European authority may be emerging, of the sort detailed in Michael Keating's contribution to the Constitutional Unit's *Scottish Independence*, and borne out by the French left's success in the regional elections.[9]

The coincidence of a European crisis and the breakdown of Britain could prove a unique opportunity for synergy, and in the immediate future.

Resolving the political crisis

Britain's deficiencies have been concealed by Anglo-Saxon globalisation getting its own way, because a hyper-rich finance-capital sector has made up its own rules and paid to have them broadcast. This has reached its limit. Financial misbehaviour plus a panicky dash for oil by the same cast members, obsessed by MacKinder's old 'heartland' paradigm, is bringing matters to a crunch.

With the ousting of the neolibs by the neocons, the soi-disant 'progressive' thrust of globalisation has been weakened, and replaced by Euro–American confrontation, not just over Iraq: Airbus may prove even more critical. With the USA and Britain bogged down in the Middle East, the balance seems likely to shift back to the Old Europe of pre-1989, dominated by France and Germany and carrying with it at least the neighbouring regions in Spain, North Italy and Austria, and with the 'New Europe' becalmed. If its core functions efficiently, it will win the confidence of the accession states. With

Blair–Brown facing a hard landing, Scotland can fortunately play two picture cards to get taken on board.

The first card is oil, a Scottish resource presently ignored. It was not the panacea it was cracked up to be in the 1970s, because it brought its own penalties, which might have been forecast by studying Scots shipbuilding and engineering from 1860 to 1920. The Clyde essentially built the delivery systems for energy, ie coal – machinery, railways, ships – on which industrialisation depended until the Second World War, and their 'Upas Tree effect' absorbed or priced out the resources which might have produced a more balanced economy. The 1970s were similar, though social-democratic Norway planned its way out. Still, we got some sort of social dividend from it, and it didn't corrupt the state. Nigeria, by contrast, was simply pillaged by the companies in cahoots with a venal élite, and the same is likely to occur in the ex-USSR.

In early 2005 any fluctuations in oil price have gone. In 1996 the US Delphi Institute was forecasting the US$20 barrel for 2016; when Scotland voted in 1999, North Sea production (at its all-time peak of 3 million barrels per day (mbd)) was yielding under $10 dollars a barrel, or about $11 billion per annum. This did no favours for the SNP. But in 2004 the price went from $33 a barrel, dragging in $23 billion, to upwards of $50. Middle Eastern instability and Chinese industrialisation are still pushing the price up, so even with a forecast decline in North Sea output to 1.3 mbd in 2010 (though likely to be checked by new technology which prolongs the life of fields), there is still, for Scotland, a lot of money to be played for – given a $40 barrel is about $19 billion a year.

The other card is Trident. Old Europe is in nuclear terms underarmed, and Scotland is the reluctant custodian of the British deterrent. The SNP and points left want the Royal Navy's nukes away from the Clyde. Professor William Walker and Dr Malcolm Chalmers, respectively of St Andrews and Bradford, have argued that without Faslane and Coulport the expense of relocating the submarines at English ports would force them to revert to America, leaving Britain a non-nuclear power. A Scots bid for independence could use Trident as a bargaining-point, compelling Britain to pool its deterrent with Europe or even, in the last resort, to offer direct Scots–European negotiation over the future of nuclear arms.

To move from the rather large pretendy Parliament of Jack McConnell to the Great Game seems vertiginous. Scotland is in a situation, however, where both national self-interest and the good of a stable world order – things that have combined fatefully in earlier epochs – have again coincided, in the shape of a revived balance of power and the promise of a renewed European autonomy. The Auld Alliance is back, and it's alluring.

Christopher Harvie has been Professor of British and Irish Studies at the University of Tubingen in Baden-Württemberg, Germany. He is the author of several books including No Gods and Precious Few Heroes, *and his latest is* Mending Scotland: essays in economic regeneration.

Notes

1 R Dahrendorf, 'Towards the 21st century' in M Howard and LW Roger (eds), *The Oxford History of the Twentieth Century* (Oxford: Oxford University Press, 1998), p 338.
2 C Harvie, *The Rise of Regional Europe* (London: Routledge, 1993).
3 J Sillars, *Scotland: the case for optimism* (Edinburgh: Polygon, 1986).
4 G Brown (ed), *The Red Paper on Scotland* (Edinburgh: Edinburgh University Student Publications Board, 1975).
5 A Oswald, Interview in *Guardian*, 8 May 2004.
6 J Rifkin, *The Age of Reason* (London: Penguin, 2000).
7 HM Enzensberger, 'The Italianisation of Europe', in *Europe, Europe* (London: Hutchinson Radius, 1989).
8 T Nairn, *Faces of Nationalism* (London: Verso, 1997).
9 M Keating, 'Socialism, territory and the national question', in G Hassan (ed), *The Scottish Labour Party: history, institutions and ideas* (Edinburgh: Edinburgh University Press, 2004).

17. The Authentic Tourist

How the past keeps coming back

Ian Yeoman, Mandy Brown and Una McMahon-Beattie

The historian Eric Hobsbawm observes that the past is a permanent part of human conscious.[1] It is this attachment to the past that sees past events of Scottish tourism re-occurring in the future. The tourist industry should remember why Scotland was an attractive destination in previous centuries if it is to continue to offer authentic experiences that are distinctively Scottish.

There are a number of striking ways in which the present tourism industry echoes the past. We are seeing budget airline carriers as the main drivers of tourism growth across the UK, but it must be remembered it was the railway and steamship companies that transformed Scottish tourism in Victorian times. Communities across Scotland found themselves swelled by visitors to three or four times their normal size.

Travellers worrying about crime and terrorism is not new either. The destruction of the World Trade Center reminded us that security concerns have been displaced to other destinations. Scotland in the early nineteenth century had established a reputation as a safe haven, in contrast to other parts of Europe, including Ireland, which were seen as barbaric and hostile places. In fact, Scotland was a place where young men would not fall into sexual temptation, thanks to the rule of the Kirk, and travellers were unlikely to be mugged.

Climate change is having an impact upon the Scottish tourism industry; in particular the ski industry is facing certain death and most visitors associate Scotland with rain, more rain and *dreich* days. This is nothing new; during the mid 1850s, newspaper reporters such as John Hope were extending their coverage of the weather from big cities to the resorts, and forecasts had an impact on the impulsive traveller.

Hay writes that health and spa tourism is a trend that many tourists are following.[2] Tourists turn to spa treatments for relaxation and to beat the stresses of modern daily life. In Victorian times, tourists turned to health either by the way of a cure or tonic. It was hydropathic establishments and their 'water cure' as found at Peebles, Crieff and Craiglockhart that drew increasing numbers of visitors. It was this combined with a therapy of golf and exercise that was central to the perception of 'Scotland for health'.

Moving into the future: experience, cultural capital and authenticity

If Hobsbawm is correct that the past is a representation of the future, what are the long-term prospects for Scottish tourism?

Durie notes that tourism has flourished in Scotland since Victorian times and is an industry with an everlasting future.[3] One thing is certain; tourism will be here in 2020 and beyond. The current picture is healthy. Scotland's tourist industry is worth £4.5 billion annually. It represents 5 per cent of gross domestic product (GDP) and employs 8 per cent of the working population. Tourism is an industry that cannot be outsourced to India or China, as are financial services and call centres. It is an industry that will last longer than oil and gas when these resources are exhausted. More importantly, it is an industry that represents the nation's identity, values and culture.[4] It is this identification of the past and culture that will be of benefit in the future.

People are looking for new meanings from their consumption of goods and services in a way that is consistent with Maslow's self-actualisation concept. The desire for self-actualisation is a search for a wider meaning and sense of worth beyond material possessions. That can mean holidays, eating out and theatre, but also includes special experiences such as white-water rafting or spending a weekend at a health spa. We are increasingly living in an 'experience economy', where service providers have to stage an experience for consumers that goes beyond basics.[5]

The critical currency of this world of experience is cultural capital.[6] Our knowledge of culture and leisure activities helps to define who we are and, critically, differentiate us from others because we can talk authoritatively about opera, wine or even *Big Brother*. Rifkin argues we are moving from an era of industrial to cultural capitalism where 'cultural production increasingly becomes the dominant form of economic activity'.

As the experience economy matures,[7] a shift is identified in which authenticity has cultural capital. Authenticity emerges as a selection criterion tomorrow's consumer. Authenticity means that consumers centre on the pure experience that isn't tainted by copycats and they search for a truly authentic experience, which is not Hollywood and false but steeped in culture and history. With its roots in offering experiences of culture and countryside, Scotland's tourist industry is well placed to exploit this modern quest for authenticity. So how will these elements help shape the future of tourism?

Experiences

The desire for escapism and activities is well established within Scottish tourism. The growing trend for alternative lifestyles, concerns about food supply and obesity lead to a desire for health, activity and well-being. The development of spa tourism is well-established in mainland Europe. These consumers are high-spending with high expectations.

Scotland's provision of hydropathic spa services will lead to a product that will link beauty and anti-ageing to health spa treatments. The concern for diet and food supply will facilitate more farmers' markets and food tourism based upon natural and local food produce. Concerns about obesity and anti-ageing will drive the sport and activities markets.

Traditional activities such as walking and cycling will be supplemented with soft adventure sports such as white-water rafting and abseiling. Destinations such as Perthshire and Arran will become known as Adventure Sports playgrounds. Many of these activities will focus on the weekend leisure visitor, where activities are hobbies combined with holidays.

An awareness of Scotland as a high-quality environment is well established. The promotion of Scotland as a green tourism and environmentally friendly destination is essential. For example, the changes in behaviour of German citizens in refuse sorting and collection means that these consumers specifically seek out green tourism accredited products. The trait is now conditioned into many sophisticated consumers to the extent that a concern for the environment leads to conservation style holidays, in which tourists repair dry stone walls in local communities in order to 'feel good'.

Cultural capital

The continued trend of a highly educated population is one that is shaping the cultural sector. As we talk about the 'arts', we reflect upon the role of culture in society as a means to fulfil ourselves. The rise of the entertainment economy is an accumulation of experiences. From a tourism perspective it means hobbies as activities and cultural festivals.

Scotland is well associated with cultural capital. Edinburgh is one example of a festival destination which includes the International Festival, the Fringe, jazz and blues, television, film or hogmanay.[8]

Traditional art forms include dance, for instance that performed by the Scottish Ballet, and the visual arts, such as what is shown at the National Galleries. Whether catering for an interest in Celtic culture, ie the Mod, or celebrity spotting at the MTV Awards, Scotland offers a diverse cultural experience from heritage to modern. The interest in hobbies, eg reading, has resulted in Wigtown being nominated as a 'book town'; there is also the artists' town, Kirkcudbright, for art appreciation. Both towns are popular weekend break destinations.

Authenticity

Lennon points out that those destinations that can distinguish themselves through strong icons will survive the phenomena of international growth in tourism over the next 20 years.[9] These icons give Scotland high icon value to consumers all over the world. Its history of tartan, golf, whisky, heritage, breathtaking landscapes, festivals, monsters, Isles and cities makes Scotland an authentic experience that cannot be manufactured. Holidays that focus on the real Scotland, such as activities of tracing your roots and ancestors, is now a major hobby that is shaping tourism.

Nowhere else in the world is tartan associated with a country. The kilt is unique to Scotland and is recognised all over the world. The Edinburgh Military Tattoo continues to sell out every year, six months in advance. It is the combination of the castle venue and tartan, bagpipes and drums with Scotland's military history that makes the Edinburgh Tattoo such an iconic event with international appeal.

Whisky is one of Scotland's leading exports. Its alliance with tourism is evident, whether through a tour of distilleries, a visit to the Whisky Heritage Centre in Edinburgh, the whisky trails in Speyside or simply enjoying decent single malt after dinner. The authenticity and remoteness of Scotland's Isles is something that hasn't been spoilt by the trappings of a modern world. Destinations like the Orkney and Shetland Isles offer tranquillity and solitude away from the hustle and bustle of daily life. Scotland's cities offer a richness of history, whether it is a Georgian New Town of Edinburgh or Stirling's castle and Wallace monument.

Conclusion

There is truth in Hobsbawm's philosophy that history does repeat itself, as history does repeat itself.[10] The importance of such a saying is that tourism is a representation of Scotland's identity that can't be taken away. Those that have responsibility for tourism today must ensure that the past is conserved in order that those in future can see it and imagine it.

Ian Yeoman is Scenario Planner at VisitScotland, Mandy Brown is a product analyst at VisitScotland and Una McMahon-Beattie is a lecturer at Ulster University.

Notes

1   E Hobsbawm, *On History* (London: Weidenfeld and Nicholson, 1997).
2   B Hay, 'A vision of tourism in 2020' in N Hood, J Peat, E Peters and S Young (eds), *Scotland in a Global Economy: the 2020 vision* (Basingstoke: Palgrave, 2002).
3   A Durie, *Scotland for the Holidays: tourism in Scotland 1780–1939* (Edinburgh: Tuckwell Press, 2003).
4   IS Yeoman, 'What do you want Scottish tourism to look like in 2015?', *Economic Quarterly Commentary* 29, no 2 (2004): 31–47.
5   JB Pine, BJ Pine II and JH Gilmore, *The Experience Economy* (Boston: Harvard Business School Press, 1999); M Willmott and W Nelson, *Complicated Lives: sophisticated consumers, intricate lifestyles and simple solutions* (Chichester: Wiley, 2003).
6   J Rifkin, *The Age of Access* (London: Penguin, 2000); P Bourdieu, *Distinction: a social critique of the judgement of taste* (London: Routledge, 1984).
7   J Pine II, 'The authentic experience', Travel and Tourism Research Conference, Montreal, June 2004.
8   E Miller, *Edinburgh International Festival 1947–1997* (Edinburgh: Scolar Press, 1996).
9   J Lennon, 'Benchmarking Scottish tourism against international competition' in *Looking East* (Edinburgh: VisitScotland, 8 Oct 2004).
10   Hobsbawm, *On History*.

18. The Myth of the Egalitarian Society and the Equality Debate

Are we really Jock Tamson's bairns?

Rowena Arshad and Elinor Kelly

The story so far...

However one examines the state of Scottish society and the issue of equality, we have come far in the last five years. Scotland has lived through a period of remarkable hope, action, activism and energy from a range of players – from parliamentarians to leaders, activists and campaigners in civic Scotland for change, improved participation and representation, and an end to prejudice, bigotry and discrimination.

Devolution has given Scotland the ability to establish a national framework for action which has equality and justice as one of its cornerstones. And diversity has now joined social inclusion in the leading refrains of political chorus. Some of the most memorable moments in progressing equity in Scotland have been when individuals have dared to speak out, eg James MacMillan's 'Scotland's shame' speech,[1] which legitimised discussions publicly on anti-Catholic sectarianism and religious bigotry. Another case was when the Labour Party pushed forward its repeal of Clause 28/Section 2A, which was the bar on local authorities to 'promote' homosexual 'pretended' family relationships.

That is one version of Scotland over recent years, and one with much credence and evidence. Another viewpoint questions how much our new parliamentary classes, political institutions and civic agencies have actually changed. This sees devolution as having widened the number and range of public agencies to include an equality discourse, but stopping short of transferring power from existing frameworks into the hands of people.

The story of equality debates in Scotland has been long, acrimonious and controversial, filled with myth, folklore and a sense of nervousness about public debate. One story, shaped by the moral authoritarian or guardian view of Scotland, has seen the Parliament foist a politically correct orthodoxy on a conservative nation via such measures as the already mentioned Clause 28, banning fox hunting and the proposed smoking ban. Another view shaped by the primacy of class politics sees economic discrimination as the main dividing line of inequality in Scotland and wider equality debates as the preserve of the professional middle class. And then there is the popular belief of Scotland as an open, egalitarian country: the land of Jock Tamson's bairns, where social mobility and prejudice are supposedly less important issues than for our southern neighbours. Finally, there is the 'official' version of Scotland, which stresses that by slow, incremental change, it is possible to make significant progress, build alliances and consensus, and not threaten old or new elites.

This simplified summary of discourse on equality indicates that a more far reaching and fundamental perspective, which gives voice and power to those who are excluded, powerless or who have directly faced discrimination, has mostly although not entirely been missing from the debate.

The languages of socially inclusive Scotland

In line with many other nations around the world, Scotland's efforts to decrease social inequality and to 'manage' diversity has relied on a range of social policies, most of which are under the control of the Scottish Parliament. As we take stock and move to the next stage of the life cycle of this devolved nation, we need to reflect critically on efforts to date so that we are better informed about the future Scotland we want.

The Scottish approach to tackling social exclusion is differentiated from the wider British framework by naming the Scottish programme *social inclusion*. This was meant to signify Scotland's positive approach to exclusion issues and for the politicians and policy-makers not to be a mere exercise in nomenclature. However, Saloojee reminds us that 'the utility of the concept of social inclusion will depend on the extent and degree to which it successfully deals with social exclusion and the extent to which it promotes social cohesion in a society that is fractured along numerous fault lines'.[2]

Equality practitioners, community workers and activists in the field find that those who are disempowered continue to wish to speak about disempowerment. Yet those who are in power are more likely to wish to concentrate on dialogues that are more positive and generate a feeling of progress. They are frustrated by a 'whinging' civic Scotland, seemingly incapable of appreciating how much has been 'done for them'. Any criticism by those outwith those in power is frowned upon and those who complain are reminded not to have such a short memory of a Scotland pre-devolution when the few dominated over the majority.

Yet, it is important to be able to name and source problems if solutions are to be sought. In the area of race equality, for example, this would mean identifying forms of racism, using the terminology of anti-racism, rather than talking in 'soft and woolly' terms such as inclusion, diversity or multiculturalism. Where there are class inequalities, we should specify this, rather than talk about poverty.

For the language and practice of social inclusion to be meaningful, those who make decisions must include those who are shut out, fully or partially. It is not sufficient for those in power to feel content that their decisions are the correct ones provided they are articulated within equality principles. One of the early exercises in inclusion by Jackie Baillie, then Deputy Minister for Communities, was to establish the Racial Equality Advisory Forum (REAF) in 2000. This was a forward-thinking initiative by Baillie and the effects of this forum continue some years on. Although it could have been improved, it is the kind of participative democracy that Scotland deserves.

Being human: building human and social capital

Social inclusion does not just happen organically through policy changes. It also relies on a complex kaleidoscope of individuals, social groups and institutions that exist within the nation to collaborate, engage in dialogue and take responsibility. If these complex relationships are not nurtured, sustained and most importantly included within the processes of decision-making, then social inclusion initiatives from government are likely to have limited effectiveness.

If we are to look to the future and envisage a more equitable and democratic Scotland, then we have to introduce a governance structure distinct from government to assist this complex kaleidoscope. This governance structure would identify factors that would assist as well as hinder such maintenance. It should not shy away from those who might be less inclined to toe the government line or to praise the Executive.

Public policy will play an important role in this. To aid it, we need to ask if current policies assist the development of trust and cooperation within social groups and communities or impede them. Do policies encourage strong bonding and bridge-building between those who transcend various social divides or do policies fragment these groups causing different voices to pursue narrow interests and actively exclude others?

We would suggest that the current climate, which encourages groups and organisations (particularly those in the voluntary sector) to compete for short-term funding, does not aid bridge-building. Instead, it is an alienating mechanism that is destroying the human and social capital across diverse communities. Agencies and individuals are competing with each other through one-sided, top-down directives and programmes that are headlined under the banners of 'open competition', 'best value' and 'value-added'. The decision to fund is often in the hands of those who do not carry the work out on the ground or come from the communities the funding is often set aside to assist. The short-termism that plagues both statutory and voluntary sectors sees the loss of staff with knowledge and skills and the loss of networks built up by such initiatives. This does not bode well for sustainability on matters of inclusion and diversity.

We would argue that it is critical that a wider, civic Scotland is far more involved as active agents in policy and social capital formation. These involvements have to negotiate geographical, social, ethnic and other variations. A one-size-fits-all policy and programme design will not be optimum, and we need to guard against a 'central belt Edinburgh/Glasgow "roll out" to the rest of Scotland' mentality. Instead of short-term projects, how can the Executive and Parliament work with a wider Scotland to build on the capacity and support of local people, communities and organisations so that the diversity and inclusion programmes are not dependent on the whims of political parties and therefore election cycles?

Futures Scotland: who defines and who decides?

In advancing a future Scotland, we need to ask who should be at the decision-making tables and who needs to vacate their seats. One of the areas that requires exploration relates to the French sociologist Bourdieu's questioning of elites and their ability to call upon their social networks to reinforce and reproduce their privileged status.[3] Post-devolution, do we have a new elite in Scotland, perhaps just a tad more diverse in terms of gender, faith, disability and ethnicity?

Who are these new people seemingly with the right credentials to maintain power and do those who are excluded feel detached and disconnected from those who have these credentials? Parry identified several types of powerful governance groups in Scotland, from the political elite (elected members), to the civil service elite to leadership in public bodies (quangos).[4] Parry suggests that they come from backgrounds including academia, business, the judiciary and faith institutions. The new elite we are referring to has footholds in all these sectors but within each there has been some attention paid to issues of diversity and inclusion. For example, 2.8 per cent of Scotland's public appointments (686 in total) are from ethnic minority backgrounds and 2.3 per cent are people with disabilities. These are significantly higher figures than pre-devolution. The Scottish Parliament has 51 women MSPs out of 129, and three 'out' gay members. However, there remain, after two elections, no visible ethnic minority members of the Scottish Parliament, no increase of ethnic minority representation at local government level and an invisibility for ethnic minority representation in many strata of Scottish society such as heads of corporations (public, voluntary or private sector).

The characteristics of this new elite are their desire to be open and inclusive, to be seen to be supporting inclusion for all and a desire to develop a Scotland that closes the opportunities gap. However, less attractive characteristics might include an air of smugness that 'they know best', complacency that leads to stagnation at the 'promissory' rather than implementation level and a false sense of achievement that leads to self-exoneration rather than critical self-evaluation.

Nevertheless, we would suggest that efforts to deliver on social inclusion have been tangible and compelling. There are Scottish parliamentarians, those within the civil service and other governance frameworks who dare to speak the language of oppression, seeking to enable the marginalised to have a voice. However, we would suggest that these remain a relatively small, highly visible and vocal cabal. Though the majority of those in government now speak the language of inclusion and diversity many continue to fail fully to understand how this should affect their practices and outlooks systematically. Diversity is welcomed as long as it does not threaten the known way of life and character of our society. We have heard women speak of glass ceilings, and we are now hearing the same from ethnic minorities (visible and not visible). Is it a case of 'diversity and inclusion – this far but no further'? There is a potential tension here that needs resolution if cynicism is not to set in.

A different kind of Scotland?

Governments need to ensure that any transformation, no matter how laudable, is tolerated by the populace so that change for greater social justice is seen and felt as a process of construction rather than turbulence. Equally, solutions would be simple if there were one or two identifiable groups that are excluded. The difficulty is that groups can be both included or excluded depending on the context and issue. As it is impossible to consult everyone, selection takes place and we return to representative structures.

For future progress, there is a need to move away from the dominant format of representative structures to increasingly participative democratic structures. The role of government whether central or local would be to develop a facilitative and supportive role that helps coordinate people-directed actions and solutions.

Participative democracy occurs in pockets all over Scotland and those involved in renewing local democracy and community regeneration would argue this is happening already. We would argue that there are few examples where people, not lobbies, not big businesses, not politicians, have the final say when they choose to assert themselves.

Evidence from the Widening Access into Local Government Progress Group[5] indicates that there is a great deal of activism within Scottish communities but these energies are disengaged from traditional party political forms of representation and absent from corridors of power. Community regeneration is fine as a start but there also need to be programmes that assist this activism into governance.

Scotland has made remarkable progress over the last few years, but there is no room for self-congratulation. Taboos have been broken, and prejudice challenged. The Clause 28/Section 2A debate witnessed a public conversation about homosexuality – a first in modern Scotland.[6] We have seen a wider debate engendered by James MacMillan's 'Scotland's shame' speech on anti-Catholicism and the extent of sectarianism in society. The profile and success of campaigning groups such as Nil by Mouth in this still contentious field is proof of that. Even in areas of acute political tension there are grounds for optimism. The reaction of local communities and people to the death of Firsat Yildiz, a Turkish asylum seeker in Sighthill, was a powerful one: building alliances in solidarity with asylum seekers and anti-racism. The campaign to close Dungavel, the Home Office detention centre in South Lanarkshire which has imprisoned asylum seekers (adults and children), has crossed the political spectrum.[7]

Something significant is happening here that 'official' Scotland's view of equality and inclusion barely understands. On some issues, such as sectarianism, the Scottish Parliament and Executive have been progressive and shown leadership, but in other areas, they have lost their nerve – the Clause 28 debate being one example. In others such as Dungavel they have embraced the politics of reaction and abrogated their responsibility. And we cannot talk about equality in Scotland without mentioning the authoritarian New Labour Home Office powers on asylum seekers, ID cards, the war on terror and Belmarsh Prison. As long as politicians are prepared to use xenophobia on issues such as race, asylum and immigration, progress towards equality will be patchy.

If we take the long view, it is true that diversity is rapidly increasing in Scotland, while economic and social inequalities widen. This is a feature not just for Scotland but also for many (though not all) OECD countries. Responding to all of this, we need governance structures that will foster networks and build bridges. The coming generations in Scotland should celebrate the progress already made, but acknowledge that we still have a long road to navigate. This will involve difficult debates about the role of politicians, the powers of the Scottish and UK Parliaments, and the make up of society and civic Scotland. A Scotland more at ease with equality would be a country more at ease with itself, more diverse, and one that would welcome change. This would be a country, which in its practice of citizen's rights and empowerment, and in the creation of a culture of equality and anti-discrimination, would set a powerful and persuasive example to others. This would be a place that had embarked on a different story, and found a distinct voice.

Rowena Arshad is Director of the Centre for Education for Racial Equality in Scotland at the University of Edinburgh, and is writing in a personal capacity. Elinor Kelly is a research fellow in race and ethnic issues at the University of Glasgow.

Notes

1   James MacMillan's speech 'Scotland's shame' was given at the 1999 Edinburgh International Festival Lecture, and is included in T Devine (ed), *Scotland's Shame?: bigotry and sectarianism in modern Scotland* (Edinburgh: Mainstream, 2000).

2   A Saloojee, *Social Inclusion, Citizenship and Diversity* (Ottawa: Canadian Council on Social Development/Laidlaw Foundation, 2001); available at: www.ccsd.ca/subsites/inclusion/bp/as.htm, p 1.

3   P Bourdieu, 'The forms of capital', in JG Richards (ed), *Handbook of Theory and Research for the Sociology of Education* (New York: Greenwood Press, 1986), pp 241–58.

4   R Parry,' Leadership and the Scottish governing classes' in G Hassan and C Warhurst (eds), *Tomorrow's Scotland* (London: Lawrence and Wishart, 2002), pp 141–53.

5   See www.scotland.gov.uk/Topics/Government/local-government/18375/15788. The group submitted their report to the Tom McCabe Minister for Finance and Public Service Reform in December 2004.

6   Male homosexuality was decriminalised in England and Wales in 1967, but not until 1980 in Scotland. There was little public debate at the time in Scotland due to a number of factors: an embarrassed Conservative government, a nervous Scottish Labour Party.

7   See www.closedungavelnow.com/

19. The Future of Scottish Football

Time for a new story?

Stephen Morrow

Scottish football is not in the best of health. While the immediate aftermath of one of the national team's poorest ever results – the 1–1 draw in Moldova in a 2006 World Cup Qualifying tie – is perhaps not the ideal time to consider the future of Scottish football, of more concern is that such a result can scarcely be described a shock. Off the field Scottish football is in little better condition. Competent administration of one of the fundamental principles of sporting competition – promotion and relegation – seems annually to be beyond those charged with running Scotland's top division, while the very existence of many of our top clubs remains uncertain. Of course there have been some bright spots: notably Celtic's 2002/03 UEFA Cup Final appearance as well as the presence of two Scottish clubs in that same season's UEFA Champions' League group stages. Yet even the bright spots mask wider gloom: almost one in every two fans who attends a match in Scotland goes to watch either Celtic or Rangers at home.

The story of Scottish professional football has been shaped by a number of factors over the last century: a major football country as a neighbour; the Old Firm of Celtic and Rangers; administrative structures and objectives; ownership and finance; the teachers' strike of the mid-1980s; the widespread sale of playing fields; Bosman; social change; poor diet; even the weather. Some of these continue to be relevant and others less so. The story of Scottish football is like a journey: some factors that acted like road signs directing it forward are now more like roundabouts from which the game is finding it difficult to locate an exit route. Others need to be recognised for what they are, dead ends: myths that do not explain our lack of progress when compared with other countries. What is certain is that both types of obstacle need to be bypassed if the Scottish football story is to continue to have meaning.

The key to a more positive future for the Scottish game is radical structural change centred on inclusivity in decision-making and the policy process. This will require an open debate led by the governing body (Scottish Football Association, SFA), but involving other stake-holders as well – club directors, players, player representatives like the Scottish Professional Footballers Association (SPFA), supporter associations and trusts, sponsors, TV companies and others – about the way forward. And such a debate must be comprehensive and far-reaching leaving no sacred cows unexamined and no vested interests unchallenged.

All roads south?

In the professional era, football in England and Scotland has operated independently: separate leagues, separate national sides and separate voices within UEFA and FIFA.[1] But notwithstanding this independence, it is indisputable that England and English football has been a major explanatory factor in both the development and current condition of Scottish football.

Scottish clubs followed the English lead in terms of organisational structure, for the most part adopting the form of limited liability companies. Normally the limited liability model results in a separation of ownership and control of the company, but in football the two often continued to overlap with many Scottish clubs being owned by small groups of businessmen and a few hundred small shareholders, mostly fans. To this day most Scottish clubs are still structured as private limited companies which means that no public market exists in their shares. In effect the adoption of limited liability structure resulted in a division being created between those who owned and ran the clubs and those who supported them. Certainly there has been a broadening of ownership at a number of clubs in recent years; nevertheless, most Scottish clubs remain undercapitalised. They continue to have highly concentrated ownership structures and have restrictions on the transferability of shares.

On the playing side, until the last decade or so it was common for top Scottish players to play for English clubs – from the so-called 'Scotch professors' of the late 1800s through to players like Denis Law, Billy Bremner and Kenny Dalglish in more recent times. The presence of so many Scots in English club sides was also an influential factor in promoting supporter interest in English football north of the border. Another factor was television: long before armchair supporters had the opportunity to watch FA Premiership matches live in their own home, highlights of English football were available on terrestrial television in Scotland on Saturday nights.

At present there are 42 senior football teams in Scotland – 12 full-time teams playing in the Scottish Premier League (SPL) and a further 30 teams, the majority part-time, playing in one of the three divisions run by the Scottish Football League (SFL) (ten teams in each). The Premier League was set up in 1975/76 initially under the auspices of the SFL. Further change took place in September 1997 when Scotland's ten Premier Division clubs notified the SFL of their intention to resign and establish a new SPL in time for the 1998/99 season, a move approved by the SFA's Council and Members. The model for this change? The highly successful English Premiership – the driving force being the desire to increase the financial rewards available to top clubs particularly through improved television deals. The new league was designed to be the bright new future for Scottish football. But, at its inception and subsequently, many observers considered it as little more than a wolf in sheep's clothing: the same clubs, the same competitive imbalance, the same Old Firm dominance.

Old Firm, new market?

> *In fact I didn't know there were any other teams than Rangers*
> *and Celtic. When we kicked a tanner ball about . . . somebody*
> *was Rangers and somebody was Celtic. If I had been able to spell*
> *the word, I would have called it the great Glasgow dichotomy.*
>
> Clifford Hanley, 1976[2]

The key to understanding Scottish football is to grasp the significance – financial, social and cultural – of the so-called 'Old Firm' of Celtic and Rangers. On the field, since its inception in 1975/76, the Premier League (then the SPL) has been won by one of the big two in 25 out of 29 seasons. The first season of the Scottish League, 1890/91, saw the title shared by Dumbarton and Rangers. Since then on only 18 occasions out of a possible 107 has a club other than the Old Firm been crowned champion.[3]

The dominance of these two clubs is also apparent off the field of play. In 1890, Celtic's annual gate receipts of £5,000 were unrivalled in the UK. Among Europe's big clubs, Celtic and Rangers continue to draw a disproportionate share of their turnover directly from gate money. For example, Celtic's appearance in the 2002/03 Deloitte and Touche/Sport Business Rich List was due primarily to its 53,500 season ticket holders who help the club earn 50 per cent of its revenue on match day – the highest of any of the clubs in the top 20. Of course there are two factors for this: first, the high attendances themselves, and, second, the low value of television rights in Scotland, relative to clubs from other countries with clubs represented in the Rich List. Celtic and Rangers thus find themselves in something of a cleft stick: at a competitive disadvantage in Europe due to restricted television revenues, yet financially dominating the other clubs in the SPL, enjoying between them nearly 70 per cent of the combined turnover of the SPL clubs. On the one hand a mid-ranking club in the English Premiership will earn at least £20 million more per annum from domestic television deals than Celtic or Rangers; on the other hand the differential between domestic match day receipts at Celtic or Rangers and other SPL clubs is a similar sum per annum, leaving the SPL highly imbalanced in financial and consequently sporting terms.

New goals for Scottish football

If Scottish football is to retain its social significance well into this century, leadership, realism and common sense are required. Looking first at the clubs, notwithstanding the peculiarities of the football business, financial management and risk management need to be improved. Football clubs are not the only organisations that exist in rapidly changing environments. One responsibility of any company's directors is to respond to alterations in market conditions and to manage their business risk. In recent seasons many clubs have given the impression of disregarding financial consequences. Whether self-inflicted or otherwise, the duty of the directors is to respond appropriately to the changed financial circumstances of their industry. It is to be hoped that recent experiences at Dundee, Hearts, Livingston, Motherwell and Rangers, for example, have finally convinced directors that clubs can no longer continue to live far beyond their means.

While ultimately it is the responsibility of individual clubs to manage their business and sporting risks, some regulation of football finance and governance by the football authorities is required. The club licensing system introduced by the SFA is a positive development which will result in improved standards of financial and business practice in clubs and create a more stable operating environment. That said, initial requirements in terms of financial matters are not unduly onerous and it is to be hoped that in due course more demanding licensing requirements will be introduced in terms of things like budget approval and liquidity monitoring. But while these changes are both necessary and beneficial for football in Scotland, in themselves they are not sufficient. The risk of focusing only on internal issues of management and control is that Scottish football ends up in a state of 'genteel and stable poverty',[4] but entirely lacking in ambition.

An oft-repeated mantra is that football in Scotland must focus on youth development. In this respect the SFA's announcement of a ten-year programme of investment in youth football and its promise to 'assume an active role in leading the development of youth football in Scotland' is a welcome, if, some might say, overdue, policy and statement of intent to deliver.[5] But it is fundamentally important that we now progress from rhetoric to action. In particular it is essential that systems are put in place to ensure there is appropriate monitoring and evaluation of the new 'Many Players – One Goal' action plan and to ensure public accountability. While a contribution to funding from the Scottish Executive for this particular initiative is to be welcomed, the wider financial context of the SFA (and its member clubs) and its ability to continue to invest heavily in development initiatives looks less promising. The repeated failure of the national side to reach the finals of major competitions inevitably has implications for the SFA's revenue generation capabilities, both directly through, for example, prize money, and indirectly, for example in terms of the attractiveness of the team to commercial organisations such as sponsors and television companies.

Furthermore, back on the field the lack of Scottish success and the absence of role models are likely to do little to encourage children to want to play football in the first place. Taken together with the poor facilities found in much of the country, persuading the next generation of players away from other leisure options will be a major task. The risk of a vicious circle of lack of success on and off field fuelling each other is only too apparent. In truth the present 'feel bad' factor surrounding Scottish football seems likely to have continuing implications.

In terms of promoting youth development, the present financial difficulties of many top clubs are something of a double-edged sword. There is a risk that clubs will adopt a short-termist attitude to youth development, viewing it as a discretionary and hence avoidable cost and thus reducing their investment in both personnel and infrastructure. It is also a concern that there still seems to be a gap between the clubs and the SFA on something as fundamental as how best to encourage and develop the young talent that is out there.

The Old Firm and the wider future

Central to the future is the role of the Old Firm. Ideally, debate about structural change in Scottish football would not take place against a backdrop of uncertainty on whether the future of these clubs lies within or beyond Scotland. The preferred option for these clubs, and very probably for other Scottish clubs, is for them to head south to participate in one of the English leagues. It is interesting to reflect that the founder of the Football League in 1888, a Scot called William McGregor, apparently envisaged just such a possibility, his ostensibly Anglo-centric title in fact reflecting his hope that in future Scottish clubs would be admitted as members. Of course, this change is not in the gift of Scottish clubs or Scottish governing bodies. That said, there seems little merit in failing to open honest dialogue between the clubs and the administrators, and just as importantly with administrators in other countries, with UEFA and with others with a responsibility for sports policy in Europe, such as the European Commission, with the aim of working towards an orderly departure from Scottish football.[6]

Ultimately, irrespective of Celtic and Rangers the domestic game requires refocusing. The SPL is not and never could be a mark two version of the English Premiership. To many observers there seems little merit in the SPL standing apart from the rest of professional football in Scotland. While the absurdity of our professional clubs' per capita ratio is often highlighted, it seems no less absurd that three separate bodies have a role in regulating the game in a country with a population of less than five million people. It is unarguable that the number and precise roles of governing bodies is another area where debate must take place with a view to change.

If the SPL is brought back into the mainstream of Scottish football, the opportunity for restructuring it and the other professional leagues then presents itself. One option is to increase the size of the top league, perhaps to 16 teams. Another is to introduce some form of regional structure, perhaps for all clubs outwith the top league, were it to be a 16-team top league, or for all clubs outwith the top two divisions if league sizes of 12 or 10 were deemed preferable. At the same time realistic regulations are required in terms of things like capacity demands and ground sharing, set within the licensing framework. When the average home SPL attendance excluding Celtic Park and Ibrox is approximately 8,000 there is no merit in placing unnecessary financial burdens on clubs in terms of facility development. Similarly, the absurdity of forcing Inverness Caledonian Thistle to play its home SPL matches in Aberdeen, remote from its community, in front of very small crowds, inevitably with negative financial consequences for the club, should never be allowed to happen. Realism and pragmatism are required. Attention should be given to fostering fairer competition on the field. While a return to the revenue-sharing schemes common in the 1970s and 1980s may seem unrealistic given the market-centred philosophy now pervasive in football, nevertheless small changes could have measurable impacts. For example, the suggestion that clubs promoted into what is presently the SPL should receive a windfall promotion gain or 'golden hello' is an attractive option that might help clubs to reduce the income gap and encourage on-field competitiveness.

Turning to ownership structure, the existing ownership models have demonstrably failed. One way forward is to broaden the ownership of clubs. For many clubs the future is dependent on repositioning themselves as community resources, encouraging supporters, the local community, local business and local councils to become integrally involved in the ownership, governance and management of the clubs. Initiatives such as Supporters Direct and its encouragement to supporters to set up mutually structured Supporter Trusts to take a stake in their clubs have already shown their value, financially and otherwise, at many clubs. Already there are trusts at 30 of the 42 senior Scottish clubs and this involvement offers some hope for the future of individual clubs. Looking at the longer term, it may be desirable for clubs to adopt more appropriate legal forms than the conventional limited liability model, which was never designed with the needs of small-scale community-based enterprises like football clubs in mind. In truth the conventional limited liability company only makes sense to many football club stakeholders if any profits are immediately ploughed back into the club. The recent creation of a new legal form for social enterprises, the Community Interest Company (CIC), presents an opportunity for clubs that have both financial and social objectives. What is envisaged is the establishment of firms that have the specific aim of benefiting the community, with any profits earned by the company being spent on community work rather than shareholders.

What these changes may provide is a better framework within which community clubs can flourish. Certainly there is an onus on clubs to demonstrate their community and social relevance and to broaden their ownership and governance. But communities – supporters and the wider community too – must respond and engage with the clubs. Whether this can happen at all 42 clubs is debateable. Unpalatable as it may be to some die-hard supporters, some clubs will disappear. No club has an inalienable right to continue in existence – history alone is not sufficient.

Other challenges exist, too, not least a great need to encourage longer-term and more balanced thinking and decision-making. Certainly the nature and organisational structure of football inevitably highlights instant success and failure. Notwithstanding this, too often football's stakeholders are guilty of unnecessary short-termism in their behaviour: undue concentration whether from the media, supporters, directors or whomever to immediate problems and immediate solutions. The haste with which so many championed Walter Smith as the replacement for Berti Vogts as the manager of the Scottish national team, irrespective of whether Smith was the most suitable candidate or had the required attributes for that particular position, is but one example of this symptom. It is somewhat paradoxical that the present poor condition of much of Scottish football may actually provide the best opportunity for encouraging such necessary attitudinal change.

Since its inception Scottish football has had a fascinating story to tell. But what is required at this juncture is a new story; one rooted not in history but in the economic and social circumstances of contemporary Scotland. It is also to be hoped that the story can be developed with an eye on the long term.

Stephen Morrow is a senior lecturer in the Department of Sports Studies at the University of Stirling and author of The People's Game? Football, finance and society.

Notes

1   B Crampsey, *The First 100 Years: the Scottish Football League* (Glasgow: Scottish Football League, 1990).

2   C Hanley, 'The Old Firm' in I Archer and T Royle (eds), *We'll Support You Evermore* (London: Souvenir Press, 1976).

3   The 18 titles have been won by: Aberdeen 4, Hearts 4, Hibernian 4, Dumbarton 1, Dundee 1, Dundee United 1, Kilmarnock 1, Motherwell 1 and Third Lanark 1.

4   Royal Commission on Gambling, *Report of the Royal Commission on Gambling*, Cmnd 7200 (London: HMSO, 1978).

5   Scottish Football Association, *Annual Review* (Glasgow: Scottish Football Association, 2004).

6   The problem of dominant clubs in smaller European domestic leagues is not unique to Scotland. Clubs from countries such as the Netherlands, Belgium, Norway and Denmark have had discussions about cross-border initiatives like the Atlantic League, which Scottish clubs have been involved in. See for example S Morrow, 'Atlantic League or North Atlantic drift?' in Singer and Friedlander's *Season Review 2000–01*, pp 43–5 (available at www.le.ac.uk/so/css/resources/sf-review/00-01/01article9.html).

20. Nairn Day

A public conversation about the future

Eddie Palmer and Matthew Horne

Introduction

Nairn Day was an experiment in creating a 'public conversation' about the future of Scotland. Its success showed that futures thinking is not only the domain of experts.

Imagine it's Scotland in 2020 and Nairn is the national capital. Perhaps that parliament building fell into a hole in the ground or global warming flooded Edinburgh up to Arthur's Seat. But it doesn't really matter how – just imagine Nairn is Scotland's new capital. With your help, we want to find out how Nairn and Scotland might look and feel different.

This invitation was sent to around 1,000 households in Nairn and the surrounding area. The *Nairnshire Telegraph* picked up the theme with a front page story headlined 'Nairn – Capital of Scotland!' With the help of the local enterprise company, Nairn Day posters were put up in libraries and public buildings throughout the town.

We wanted to find participants for a day-long event to talk about the future, which had the feel of a town meeting. The aim of the Scotland 2020 project was create a 'public conversation' about the future of Scotland; this event was an attempt to prove that it could be done.

We chose Nairn because we felt it was small enough to generate word-of-mouth awareness of the event but big enough to host such an event. We also had a hunch that this might be easier to do in a Highland town. To succeed in filling a room, we knew that we had to create a genuine buzz around the event since we were asking people to give up their Saturday to take part.

The contention of the project has been that engaging the public in a discussion about the future was both possible and worthwhile. Public engagement is generally seen as a good thing by politicians and policy-makers, but the practicalities of how to engage the public present them with difficulties.

Where do you find 'the public'? Who sets the agenda? What are the outputs? And, above all, will anyone show up?

The cynical view of public meetings is that people only show up to complain, and even then it is a self-selecting group of busybodies and serial committee-sitters. Nairn Day was offering anyone the chance to participate in a discussion about the future of their town and Scotland as a whole, but we tried to avoid pushing any of the usual Nimby buttons that are usually used to recruit a room full of people.

In fact, the event was designed without any agenda, beyond the rather fanciful request to imagine Nairn as the Scottish capital. The aim was to let participants set the agenda, and enable the issues they feel passionately about to emerge.

On 1 September 2004, participants met at the spacious and pleasant conference centre at the Newton Hotel in Nairn. Over 70 people registered to take part. They were ordinary people from Nairn, invited at random, and the composition of the room showed a genuine diversity of opinion and background.

About Open Space

Open Space is one of a family of techniques, known collectively as 'large group processes'. The technique was adapted from a traditional approach to strategic thinking and planning, and conflict resolution, in West African cultures.

The evolution of Open Space is not that surprising, given the growing interest in a more 'democratic' way of doing things, and the widespread debate of citizenship issues in the UK. During the 1960s and 1970s there was considerable enthusiasm in the development of the social psychology of groups.

Open Space can be traced to the annual conference of the American Management Association in 1982. Harrison Owen, credited with the design of Open Space, experimented with 'trying to make it all like a coffee break'. That is, creating a time when people talk to others who share an interest, enthusiasm and commitment to the same subject.

Open Space is simple and very effective. It has been used in 106 countries to date and is based upon the following set of beliefs:

O   Participants can self-organise their own event.
O   They are competent to discuss possible solutions to shared problems.
O   They can usually reach consensus on difficult subjects.
O   People do not need outside 'experts' to solve problems for them, as they have enough information at hand and, to one degree or another, are all 'experts by experience'.
O   The solutions are often are owned by everybody present, without the drawbacks of top-down 'selling' needed in organisations, because the process is open, transparent, democratic and done in real-time.
O   A large group event brings together people who have never met before on a common subject, making discussion and decisions unique to that particular group.

The following architecture of Open Space is also very important:

O   The whole group starts the day in a circle or in concentric circles to accommodate numbers.
O   Participants break into smaller group circles to work on specific issues raised in an open market place.
O   There is no 'front' or top table.

○ There is no need for any other training equipment except flipcharts and chairs in circles, which is counter-cultural to most settings.

Participants have the following options during an Open Space event, which is very different from a conventional conference. They can:

○ decide whether or not to attend and participate in a different type of event, ie the principle is 'Whoever comes are the right people'
○ raise a subject, a burning issue, in front of the whole group for discussion
○ go and join other people to discuss a subject of mutual interest
○ leave one group and join another (the 'Law of Two Feet' or 'Law of Mobility')
○ help contribute to and decide on a group's proposed action points
○ decide on preferences among all group action points by voting the priorities of the whole group.

Why does the process work? The results of the Nairn event are described below and will help the reader understand more about outputs, but the crucial point to make is that Open Space is counter-intuitive in modern Western culture. The process is driven by passion (concern over an issue) and responsibility (doing something about the issue). Participation generates commitment, because the process is open, transparent and truly bottom-up.

What came out of Nairn Day?

Physical planning issues are very important in Nairn. The town is overshadowed by the startling development of Inverness, one of the fastest growing cities in Europe. The local population is now facing an extra 10,000 people moving into an area of 12,000 currently, as well as the expansion of Inverness airport.

So, it was not a surprise that the following comment was made during the closing ceremony: 'Why do government agencies think that development is good in itself – they haven't asked us!' The comments related to specific issues for Nairn but often were linked to the kind of dissatisfaction with public bodies that would be found anywhere in Britain.

The reason we chose Nairn was because we thought that Highlanders would have a different approach to politics than the so-called political class in the central belt. They proved us right and wrong.

We were wrong in that the concerns of the people of Nairn are reflected in the political debates in Holyrood. The domestic policy issues that mattered most to the people of Nairn were actually the same issues that concern the policy-makers and politicians.

How do you integrate transport systems? How do you tackle drug abuse, crime and anti-social behaviour? How do you balance economic growth with well-being and community cohesion?

Whether you live in Nairn, Edinburgh or Lanarkshire the political agenda is shared. We made the same observation at our futures workshops in Edinburgh: Scotland has a set of issues that are everyone's concern.

But we were right in that the way the people of Nairn debated these important issues was very different from the way formal party politics approaches them:

O There were few vested interests.
O Politics was about community problem-solving rather than competition for the best idea.
O Participants were challenging without being oppositional.
O They managed their own disagreements.
O They did not try and force a consensus.
O They engaged in dialogue rather than argument.
O They sought to understand one another.
O They grappled with competing priorities.
O They recognised the interconnected nature of all these issues.

Nairn Day demonstrated the possibility of holding a public conversation about the future of a community and country that grappled with all the complexity of challenges and problems. Participants realised that there were no easy solutions, that there were difficult decisions and the need to prioritise, and that they could do this in a way that created a hunger for more debate, dialogue and action; a hunger for more politics, not less.

Our conclusion is that giving people the tools and space to be their own politicians enables them to participate directly in the democratic process. The experience of doing politics for themselves individually and as communities offers a constructive alternative to complaining about politicians.

The results of Nairn Day

We reproduce exactly what small groups write, and sometimes, as in the Nairn case, aggregate top priorities. This is how the people at the Nairn event voted for their main priorities for the future of their town.

Top ten aggregated groupings of action priorities and concerns voted by participants (number of votes)

1. Integrated and appropriate transport, including road, rail and air (146)
2. Health and social services issues – national and local (72)
3. Economic and employment issues (46)
4. Tourism, promotion and the future (45)
5. Housing, issues of second homes, holiday homes and affordable housing (40)
6. Community-building and facilities (30)
7. Families and parents (26)
8. Education issues (23)
9. Consultation of the community, and policing issues (21 each)
10. Young people's issues (19)

Top ten action priorities voted for by participants (number of votes)

1. Both A9 and A96 to be dualled, and to by-pass local communities (38)
2. Ninety-nine per cent of the local population want a by-pass for Nairn (29)
3. Better road and rail links to the airport (27)
4. There need to be opportunities at all skill levels for employment for people, especially young people (27)
5. Re-awakening of the Nairn Initiative on Tourism (26)
6. Central funding for health care in Scotland, for more equitable distribution (24)
7. Investment in nurturing and education for children – long-term, transparent and not target-led (23)
8. Put a lot of pressure on government to build a new road from Inverness to Aberdeen – dual-carriageway all the way (22)
9. Responsibility of parents and guardians to educate, not only inform (20)
10. Quality of life in Nairn; impact of youth; in schools develop understanding of what kids want for their recreation, as many opportunities for growth have gone due to over-regulation and PC – we need to address this (19)

Eddie Palmer is a director of Open Futures, an Edinburgh-based company that specialises in large group processes. Matthew Horne is a senior researcher at Demos. Nairn Day was supported by Inverness and Nairn Enterprise Company, and Highland Council. Demos and Open Futures would like to thank all the people of Nairnshire whose time and enthusiasm made the event a success.

Public conversations about Scotland

A series of discussions were held with Scottish and international thinkers. They address the links between economic growth, life satisfaction, and health and well-being. The degree of cultural change, historically and more recently is examined. And, finally, we look at Scotland's place in an interdependent world: in the United Kingdom, European Union and globalised economy.

21. Happiness, Well-being and Economic Prosperity

David Bell in conversation with Clive Hamilton

Stirling
27 September 2004

Dear Clive,
I enclose my opening gambit to you.

1. The growth record of the Scottish economy is somewhat
    below that of the UK as a whole. Nevertheless, during the
    1990s and early part of the new century, the UK has
    experienced higher rates of growth than most of the other
    G8 countries with the exception of the USA. Scottish GDP
    per capita has increased very substantially since the 1970s.
2. However, on almost all metrics, Scotland tends to
    compare its performance with that of England (or the rest
    of the UK). This has resulted in much attention being
    given to its relatively weak growth performance. Local
    policy-makers have responded by placing increased rates
    of economic growth at the top of their list of policy
    priorities.
3. The Scottish economy has a relatively large public sector
    and runs a substantial budget deficit, which is funded by
    the Westminster government. Higher rates of growth
    would play some part in reducing that deficit.

4. Scottish GDP per head is around 6 per cent below the UK average, but in fact, because income per capita in the South East is substantially higher than in other parts of the UK, GDP per capita in Scotland is higher than in most English regions, Wales and Northern Ireland.

5. Scotland has an apparently strong labour market with low rates of unemployment and some skill shortages. However, this masks high rates of absence from the workforce due to sickness or disability, particularly among older males of working age in West Central Scotland. The Scottish labour market is flexible, in the sense of offering a wide range of working time possibilities, but average working hours, particularly for men, are long by European standards, leading to the belief that Scotland is an 'income-rich time-poor' society.

6. On almost all health measures, Scotland performs poorly compared with the rest of the UK (and the developed world). Again, problems such as heart disease and cancer are particularly concentrated in West Central Scotland. Suicide rates are also high, as are rates of violent crime.

7. Levels of subjective well-being have been recorded consistently in Scotland for over three decades. These show that subjective well-being in Scotland has not increased since the early 1970s. There has been a modest improvement in England and Wales.

8. Subjective well-being in Scotland appears to be influenced by the same set of variables that have been shown to be important for other developed countries. Thus relationships and esteem in the labour market are key indicators of subjective well-being, while age and gender play the same roles that have been observed elsewhere.

9. This leads to some basic questions: Why have levels of subjective well-being not risen with higher income? What policies might actually influence well-being – or is that beyond the control of a Scottish Executive, which has

limited powers, and a generally short-term perspective? Are there common causal factors affecting both ill-health and subjective well-being at the aggregate level?

Cheers,
David

Canberra
7 October 2004

David,
Thanks for your opening contribution to this debate about growth and well-being in Scotland. Here are some initial reflections.

1. People in rich countries – such as the UK, Australia and the US – are around three times richer than their parents or grandparents were in the early 1950s yet, by any measure of happiness or well-being, they are no better off. This immediately poses the question of why governments and individuals pursue economic growth and higher incomes with such determination, often at the expense of other things.

2. One of the more disturbing aspects of this growth fetishism is the declining state of psychological health, reflected in rising rates of depression and, in some countries at least, youth suicide. Although this may be more attributable to other social and cultural changes, there is little doubt that the extraordinary emphasis on growth and income as the central measures of national and personal success has created expectations for social and individual contentment that have been disappointed.

3. The 'market freedoms' promoted by neoliberalism go hand in hand with the personal freedoms and rights

demanded by the liberation movements of the 1960s. As I have argued elsewhere, in a sense the groundwork for Thatcherism was laid by those movements (see *The Disappointment of Liberalism* under 'What's New', at www.tai.org.au). Before we could take advantage of the opportunity created by the dissolution of the bonds of conservatism, the marketers arrived with their own answer to the question: 'How should we live?'

4. The idea of happiness itself – and thus the object of life – has been redefined. People now pursue happiness by attempting to maximise the number of pleasurable episodes, defined as emotional and physical highs. This has a strong influence on how we govern our working lives, how we engage in leisure and how we think about our personal relationships. One manifestation of this is a much greater tendency to pursue short-term gratification at the expense of the 'work' necessary to develop our potentialities and the quality of our relationships. It is also manifested in rising levels of (legal and illegal) drug taking and plummeting levels of savings.

5. I suspect – and would be keen to hear other views on this – that the process of redefining life as the pursuit of highs rather than the more meaningful idea of finding fulfilment, has taken hold much more in the Anglophone countries than in continental Europe. Though it is fascinating to hear the stories from Russia and eastern Germany about the decline in social values as consumerism takes hold.

6. This redefinition of happiness has important implications for measures of subjective well-being. When asked by interviewers most people will say 'I'm reasonably happy' because saying otherwise might suggest you are a 'loser'.

    While most people say they are reasonably happy, most also believe that others are not happy and that society is not getting happier. In my view, measures of changes in the incidence of psychological disorders are a better and more objective indicator of social progress or regress.

7. The process of 'self-creation' has been captured by marketers and is associated, inter alia, with our increasing preoccupation with our own health (reflected, for example, in the huge increase in demand for complimentary medicine and the process of 'disease mongering' by pharmaceutical companies). We often feel sicker even though we are objectively healthier than ever (*pace* obesity).

Clive

Stirling
19 October 2004

Clive,

I agree that the focus on economic growth has been detrimental to other social objectives. However, if, for example, we take the pursuit of growth as a given over the last few decades, the key question it seems to me is 'What have been the consequences, intended and unintended, of the pursuit of growth at all costs?'

You mention the declining state of psychological health. I could certainly see a case that those who found it difficult to fit into a highly pressured lifestyle with high income aspirations would find it difficult to maintain a robust level of psychological health. But the evidence on this is somewhat mixed. There has been a clear upward trend in suicide rates since the 1950s. But the increase is concentrated mainly among young men. Why has this happened? Is it more to do with changing gender roles than with increasing affluence?

Suicide rates are also highest in the old Eastern Bloc countries, where perhaps expectations of a better lifestyle and greater affluence remain unfulfilled. Among the main OECD countries, there is no clear correlation between income growth and rates of suicide or depression.

One clear finding from the research is that suicide rates are often concentrated among the disadvantaged. There is also a problem of suicide 'contagion' – those who know someone who has committed suicide are much more likely to commit suicide themselves. There has been a huge concentration of suicides among young men in the Highlands during 2004, with the total number now around 35 I think.

I agree that what may be a key factor in undermining psychological well-being is unfulfilled expectations. But these expectations are not created by economic growth directly. Rather they are created in a culture dominated by a media which is happy to create dream worlds and sell the fantasy that these are places we should aspire to. However, individuals seem happy to buy into these notions. It is not the case that the media have to force the aspirations on a wholly unresponsive viewing or listening public. I have a feeling that evolution has programmed some of us with the 'aspiration' gene – which propels us to try to emulate the achievements of others, good or bad. Clearly, some cultures have not been smitten to the same extent as the post-reformation West has. They have been content with continuation of the status quo, but others have sought to advance in cultural and scientific knowledge. Economic growth is perhaps a by-product of these activities. I would be interested in your reaction to that idea.

This seems to link with your idea of the redefinition of happiness and here again I am going to show some anti-media prejudice. The notion of 'event-oriented happiness' rather than 'fulfilment' is an interesting contrast. The media exists to witness 'events' rather than the everyday and humdrum. But again, this is because of the audience's appetite for such stimulation.

I must agree with your assessment of physical health. Objectively we have never been healthier. Some of the credit for this must go to the medical advances which are part of the generation of knowledge which accompanies economic growth. But, as you say, self-reported health is becoming increasingly bad. I have looked at Labour Force

Survey data for Scotland and recent trends in what people report about all aspects of their health are extremely negative. Perhaps there is now an implicit belief, which our forbears almost certainly did not have, that we are entitled to perfect health and this has made people increasingly intolerant of minor ailments.

Look forward to your thoughts on this.
David

Canberra
22 October 2004

David,
You're right to stress that our aspirations and sense of what we need is determined by powerful – almost irresistible – social pressures, with massive resources and some of the best creative minds deployed to persuade us to feel permanently discontented. I will argue later that the refusal to feel discontented in this way becomes an act of revolt.

So modern capitalism must constantly recreate our sense of desire and then direct us to the ways in which the market (and the market alone) can satisfy these desires. The trick is that the market cannot actually satisfy the desires – in the end a tub of margarine cannot give us a happy family life. The continuation of the cycle depends entirely on the ability to repeat the trick over and over, and Western consumers have shown themselves to be willing to fall for it because they do not know what else to do.

The political consequences of the imagined deprivation of the middle classes are enormous. Despite unprecedented wealth, most people believe that they are suffering from a lack of money and political leaders respond to this. In a survey I commissioned while in the UK last year, 60 per cent of Britons, including almost half of those in the top income group, said they cannot afford to buy everything they really need ('Overconsumption in Britain: a culture of middle-class complaint?'). The results are pretty much the same for Australia.

When incomes in the UK double over the next 25 years or so, the chances are that even more will say that they cannot afford everything they need.

The reality of affluence for the great majority should be contrasted with the 'deprivation model' that the Left cleaves to. Social democrats and democratic socialists have a psychological predisposition to believe that the mass of people are suffering from material deprivation. We thrive on the imagined wretchedness of others. When the economy goes bad we feel secretly vindicated, for our reason to condemn the system is renewed. We revel in a collective *schadenfreude*. (When I made this argument some time back to a meeting of the Australian Labor Party and trade union Left it was met with outrage by some and as a 'breath of fresh air' by others.)

The implication is that while much of the Left remains hung up on the production process, in rich countries the big questions relate to consumption.

But what about the poor? We have been promised for decades that growth will solve poverty, but we still have it. I think we have to concede that we no longer lack the ability to solve poverty but the willingness. Yet our preoccupation with money, material things and the market is making us more self-focused and less willing to consider the interests of the poor and excluded. Our societies have become more selfish. As long as progressive people continue to buy the argument of economics that economic growth should be the principal focus of activity then they are ceding enormous power to capital, because capital is the creator of wealth. The Third Way effectively brings the trickle-down argument from poor to rich countries.

In this context let me flag a very big question. Most people feel strongly that our societies are marked by a decline in moral values, and they are right. They also know that there is a contradiction between their own pursuit of the good life through material acquisition and the social damage caused by materialism and the individualism of the market. The biggest and most important challenge for the left is to capture the values debate from the right. To do so will involve a fundamental rethink of the impact of the liberation movements of the 1960s and 1970s. This does not mean going back to the oppressive conservatism of the 1950s but of imagining, and then creating, a society based on values of mutuality, compassion and justice rather than one of aggressive individualism, self-centeredness and the 'ethic of consent' that governs our sexual lives.

Perhaps in the next response, I can comment on what I see as the most significant challenge to neoliberalism – and it's not the anti-globalisation movement which, in my view (for all of its admirable goals) is a dead end.

Best wishes,
Clive

Stirling
26 October 2004

Clive,
Thanks for your latest thought-provoking contribution. A few comments:

1. Clearly the characterisation of capitalism as needing to constantly re-create desire is an appealing one. How else would we justify the constant quest for economic growth? One possible answer, albeit at the political rather than the individual level, is the pursuit of power. Politicians do not criticise the growth agenda because it either (1) gives them more wealth to distribute (particularly appealing to all of a social democratic or socialist disposition) or (2) it reinforces a country's status in many ways (economically, politically and possibly militarily). For example, the UK would probably take a much less robust approach to Europe if its economy had not outperformed the European one for the last decade.

2. The argument about the need to constantly refuel material aspirations seems to ring true. But where does this need come from? Scots are no happier now than they were 30 years ago, but they probably are even more convinced now than they were then that the key to increased happiness is increased material wealth. One reason why the pressure is even greater now is the decline of organised religion, which does at least offer a different perspective on human progress.

3. I am a little puzzled by the discussion of poverty and exclusion. If we accept the argument that material wealth does not lead to fulfilment, then how do we define poverty and exclusion? It seems to me then that definitions based on material wealth fail and one rather has to focus on exclusion from the kinds of networks which might lead to a more fulfilling existence. This would seem to throw up arguments relating to our knowledge of what such networks are and what the routes into them are.

4. How can we be sure that moral values are declining? Citizens of (some) liberal democracies have realised the full implications of their actions much more than was the case in the past, eg eating tuna kills albatrosses. We have pressure groups whose existence seems to depend on pointing out these connections and does occasionally succeed in limiting immoral behaviour in pursuit of profit. Such groups never existed before – perhaps they are a reaction to the increasingly deliberate depletion of resources for profit. Private morality is also interesting – because there are wide variations across societies in the rules which appear to regulate personal interactions. A lot of this variation does not seem to be related to economic pressures.

5. While I can see the force of some of your arguments, I am still left wondering what you would suggest is the way

ahead for a small open country with a strong work ethic
(a relic of its Presbyterian past) on the edge of the world's
largest trading zone.

All the best,
David

Canberra
5 November 2004

David,
You ask: what could be the way ahead for a small open country with a
strong work ethic on the edge of the world's largest trading zone?
Sounds like Australia as well as Scotland. Incidentally, despite the
image of Australia as the land of the long weekend, Australians work
longer hours than any one else in the OECD, and certainly longer
than those in Europe.

I think the answer lies in transcending our growth fetishism. Once
we recognise that higher incomes in affluent countries are not the
road to greater national wellbeing we can demote economic growth as
the principal object of economic and social policy and focus on the
things that governments can influence which we know will improve
well-being. If we do so then all sorts of possibilities open up that are
currently closed off by our obsession with productivity, competition
and GDP. For instance, work can be structured principally to provide
fulfilment for the workers; education systems can be oriented towards
the creation of rounded human beings rather than income-earning
machines; foreign policy can be ethical rather than determined by the
interests of arms manufacturers; and we can become serious about
sustainability.

But won't the sky fall in? Japan provides an interesting example.
For at least a decade from the early 1990s the country experienced a
prolonged recession with GDP growth hovering around 0 or 1 per
cent. But the world didn't cave in on Japan. Sure there were some

problems – unemployment rose to 5 per cent. But some Japanese intellectuals argued that the recession provided an opportunity for a cultural renaissance, in which the values of consumerism could be challenged.

On the values question, certainly in Australia and the US there is a very widespread feeling that modern society suffers from a severe decline in values, which is usually interpreted as a rise in selfish individualism, narcissism and materialism and a decline in consideration for others, selflessness, sexual responsibility and more. Conservatives have tapped into this politically to very good effect (including in George W Bush's election victory in 2004). I think that as long as the left remains the captive of the 'ethic of consent' of the liberation movements it will fail to speak to the populace at a very fundamental level. Some progressive organisations in the US are thinking about this, notably the Center for A New American Dream and the Rockridge Institute (www.rockridgeinstitute.org).

The era of individualism has eroded the political foundations of social democracy. The left has traditionally based its political viewpoint on the notion of solidarity. But when people no longer identify strongly with their class, or indeed their ethnic origin or gender, what is the basis for solidarity? In other words, why should we care about others? This question demands an answer.

Finally, I want to point to the phenomenon of downshifting, that is, making a voluntary decision to reduce one's income in order to pursue things more valuable than additional income. Our surveys indicate that at least a fifth of the populations of Australia and Britain can be classified as downshifters. And they are decidedly not composed primarily of well-off, middle-aged people who can afford to take the risk. Although disparate, they share a rejection of market values, or at least they have made themselves no longer the captives of the market. In my view, they provide the basis for a new progressive politics.

Best wishes,
Clive

Stirling
10 November 2004

Clive,

Some thoughts on your last missive:

Let me come back to growth in a roundabout way. I believe there are a number of accounting rules that confront the state which are inescapable – in the medium to long term. These include the budget constraint: in the medium to long run, states cannot spend more than they raise in taxation. Where does this taxation come from? The top 10 per cent of earners pay 52 per cent of UK income tax (www.ifs.org.uk/). To maintain social cohesion, members of this group implicitly accept a social contract in which they are prepared to make large contributions to the welfare state in return for relatively small rewards. This acceptance cannot be guaranteed.

The increasing inequality of income, which underlies these disparities in tax contributions, is due to the increasing inequality of income. I would argue that the increasing inequality has arisen through globalisation and changes in technology which has led to a dramatic change in the 'goods' we now consume. In fact, we are moving towards the 'weightless' economy where what we value is often associated with entertainment and relatively transitory enjoyment. And 'weightless' goods are mainly forms of intellectual property that can by definition be traded easily on global networks, which produces massive rewards for those able to sell in these markets. Hence the increase in income inequality and what we might describe as the 'winner takes all' society.

In turn income inequality has been a driving force behind the creation of the 'aspirational society', where the many (relatively poor) are seduced by, but cannot attain, the lifestyles of the few (relatively rich). As I have mentioned in previous missives, the gap between aspirations and real outcomes has probably played an important part in keeping self-assessed well-being constant even though material wealth has improved substantially.

There is little doubt that much of what I have described above applies to Scotland. But perhaps you are not clear why I mentioned the budget constraint issue. The reason is that there is a very substantial gap between public spending in Scotland and taxes raised. This gap is the result of a political fix, rather than any demonstration of greater levels of 'need' in Scotland compared with other parts of the UK.

So I guess the bottom line is that the resource devoted to the provision of public services in Scotland substantially exceeds the ability of the Scottish economy to generate tax resources. This creates a quandary for the anti-growth arguments. A world less oriented to frantic production and more focused on personal fulfilment sounds very attractive. But how do we move from one to the other in a smooth fashion? In the absence of any international agreement to set aside the growth imperative (which seems very unlikely), can a single country (or part of a country) eschew economic growth?

From my arguments above, there would also be problems in establishing a political consensus within a state. Could it threaten the implicit social contract which means that the bulk of state services are paid for by the relatively affluent? Clearly it is this group who are probably the main drivers behind economic growth in the world at present. And it is they who would have to be won over to alternative lifestyles.

While the notion of reorienting Scottish society towards a less-growth-oriented society might seem very attractive, I guess I would want to focus on the social and political processes which would underlie that outcome. I would also be worried that Scotland's already large budget deficit would be exacerbated by putting less weight on growth, making it even more dependent on taxes paid by the relatively wealthy in the South East of England. Perhaps this is just traditional pragmatic Scottish Presbyterianism: a willingness to accept that there are potential societal benefits from shifting the focus from economic growth since material wealth is not a worthwhile end in itself, but concerned that the paths to this outcome are fraught with difficulty and risks.

This is my last contribution – I would just say that I've enjoyed the experience very much and look forward to your next message.

David

Canberra
10 November 2004

Dear David
Thanks for your last missive, which moves us to some new and contentious issues. It's hard for me to respond to the particular circumstances of Scotland so let me make some comments that apply in general to rich countries.

I worry about the argument that the ability of the state to provide services relies on the consent of the rich because they pay a disproportionate share of tax revenue. This suggests that we must lock our selves into perpetual growth because that is how they sustain the growth of their incomes. The political implication is that we must accept that the rich have us over a barrel and that social change is therefore out of the question. The environmental implications of perpetual growth, despite some degree of dematerialisation in rich countries, are also a concern.

But to get to the world view that seems to underlie this argument, I think it is no longer correct or helpful to characterise societies in rich countries as divided between the rich and the poor. I know this sounds shocking coming from the progressive side of the fence, but I think we must face the reality that capitalism has been highly successful in its own terms. The Left has always had a strong attachment to the belief that inequality divides society into rich and poor and that inequality is getting worse. I believe this 'deprivation model' of the world is now outdated and paralyses the left.

First, the middle classes with moderate to high income levels are now numerically dominant. It is very hard to argue that anything more than 20 per cent of populations of rich countries suffer material deprivation, although of course it is higher in certain regions. While material deprivation was much more prevalent in, say, the 1950s, real incomes are now around three times higher. There have been periods when income inequality has worsened (the Thatcher years in the UK) and periods when it has improved. It is simply not true to maintain that inequality will always worsen and that globalisation is the culprit. We have all been very surprised to discover in the last fortnight, on the basis of unimpeachable statistical sources, that the lowest quintile of Australians have actually done quite well under the Howard government, mostly as a result of transfers from the Federal government.

This is not to trivialise poverty; quite the reverse. The wealth of the large majority makes residual poverty all the more unconscionable. But we must abandon the trickle-down thesis that the best way to tackle poverty is to focus on higher economic growth. Growth fetishism makes us more self-focused and less concerned with the interests of the disadvantaged. We do not lack the ability to solve poverty but the willingness.

Nor do I find appealing the argument that wealthy tax-payers need to feel that they get something back in order to retain their support for the welfare state. That argument has seen an obscene growth in middle-class welfare in my country which has only reduced funding for hospitals and schools. (Incidentally, middle-class and corporate welfare provide an opportunity for substantial budgetary savings.) More importantly, though, it promotes and endorses an entitlement mentality in which citizens are characterised as grasping and self-interested, exactly as the neoliberals imagine us to be. If people are treated this way then they are more likely to act that way. If progressives must accept that the world really is populated by *homo economicus* then we should give up any hope for social change and find something more remunerative to do.

Although I am less familiar with the UK statistics, I think it is true to say that it is the broad middle classes who provide the bulk of government revenue. The top 10 per cent of income earners in the

UK may pay 52 per cent of income tax, but this is only 15 per cent of total tax revenue. The view that we should somehow be grateful and treat them gingerly because they 'consent' to a fragile 'social contract' from which they get little in return locks us in to the status quo. I would rather treat the rich as people who are often immersed by their wealth and who are searching for something more meaningful to do with their lives. This is how I speak to business audiences and I am always surprised at how well it works. I have argued, only partly tongue in cheek, that instead of cutting taxes on the rich to stimulate greater entrepreneurship and all the rest, if we set higher taxes on them then, if they behaved like the neoliberals say they would and decided to work less, their neglected families would thank us.

It is not income inequality that has created the aspirational society, but its opposite, the fact that the incomes of the bulk of the working class are now high enough for them to aspire to things that were previously out of their financial reach and were culturally inappropriate. Manufacturers have responded to this 'democratisation of luxury' with the creation of so-called entry-level products. It is not out of the question nowadays for someone on even a quite modest income to acquire a Mercedes-Benz. Check the prices of the cheapest models.

How is the transition to a post-growth society to be made? Well, I think there are signs that it is being made already. My own research on downshifting in the UK showed that 25 per cent of adults aged 30–59 had made a voluntary decision to reduce their incomes over the previous decade (the figure is 24 per cent for Scotland). They are remarkably evenly spread across age ranges and social grades (so not just middle-aged, middle-class people who can afford it). There is a summary of the report (*Downshifting in Britain: a sea-change in the pursuit of happiness?*, Discussion Paper Number 58, November 2003) on our website (www.tai.org.au).

I believe that a new progressive politics can be built on the rejection, or at least tempering, of materialism and consumerism that this trend represents. These are people who have responded to the recognition that there must be more to life than a plasma TV. We need a politics of downshifting.

I too have enjoyed our exchange. It has helped me to clarify many things.

Best wishes,
Clive

David Bell is Professor of Economics at the University of Stirling and Co-Director of scotecon, the Scottish Economic Policy Network.
Clive Hamilton is Executive Director of the Australia Institute and author of Growth Fetish *(London: Pluto Press, 2004).*

22. Scotland's 'Velvet Revolution'

Carol Craig in conversation with Tom Devine

CC: I would like to start with a general discussion about Scotland and transformational change. The author of *The Tipping Point*, Malcolm Gladwell, argues that people tend to see change as slow and incremental when in fact it is often rapid and transformatory. He argues that snow is a good example of this. When snow falls the temperature change is often minimal yet within minutes the world looks different. As a historian can you identify times in Scotland's past when change happened quickly and peoples' lives changed dramatically as a result?

TD: There are several examples but I think the most cogent is the extraordinary period in the eighteenth and early nineteenth centuries – a period which is sometimes known as the age of improvement or the age of enlightenment. The reason why this is a very telling example of what you are talking about is because elites in Scotland *consciously* agreed on a formula of modernisation.

CC: When you say elites do you mean the landowners?

TD: Correct. The landed classes. And it is one of the ironies of this story that the most progressive forces, at least in terms of material improvement, were the leaders of the old society.

CC: You said the elites were intent on a conscious transformation of Scotland. Were they deliberately trying to hold on to power or did they have a vision, or ideal, of a better society?

TD: These elites saw the process I am describing as a drive for 'improvement' – in our modern world we would call it a drive for modernisation. Whatever its name, it was a rejection of the past and an unalloyed and uncritical desire for a new type of future. Scholars regard the Scottish elites of the seventeenth and eighteenth centuries as a sordid bunch – this is what Burns meant when he talked about 'sic a parcel o rogues in a nation' – and undoubtedly greed, the desire for profit, played its part. Remember this is the beginning of the age of conspicuous consumption. It has been called a 'revolution in manners' and it cost money, hence the elite's interest in increasing revenue from their property. But the fascinating thing is this. Alongside this desire for increased profit were two other drivers. One you could almost call patriotism. A sense that Old Scotia had fallen markedly behind the power to the south – England. One part of this was not so much an uncritical admiration of England – by that stage the most dominant nation in the world – but a sense of inferiority and a feeling that Scotland had to catch up. Another driver, not directly related to profit, is the intellectual revolution which emanated from what we now call the Enlightenment. This led to the view that everything should be judged by reason. Remember a large number of the elite in Scotland went to university and this was unusual in Europe. This meant that as young men they had listened to lectures given by intellectual giants such as Francis Hutcheson, Adam Smith and David Hume. So when the type of orthodoxy started to develop which saw reason as the way forward, these elites looked round old Scotia, even their estates, and they saw chaos and anarchy.

CC: So are you saying that one motivation for their reforms was an attempt to impose order on the world round about them?

TD: Absolutely. They wanted reform and they wanted order. If you look round rural Scotland today – its neat hedgerows, roads and individualised farm houses – it is actually a product of that age. Another example can be found in the symmetry of Edinburgh's New Town. These are concrete, tangible examples of reason in action.

CC: In *The Tipping Point*, Malcolm Gladwell makes much of the idea that in large-scale transformational change it is the activity of certain individuals which is critical. He calls this 'the law of the few'.

TD: Another name for the same idea is the 'theory of Cleopatra's nose' for if she had not been so beautiful the course of history would have been different.

CC: So thinking about the Scottish Enlightenment are there people who stand out as being 'connectors' who could get the message out to a much wider audience?

TD: The fascinating thing about that period, perhaps even more than our own when we have so much technology, is that it was not only a national but also an international network. So there was constant correspondence between these men particularly in the central belt and the cities of Glasgow and Edinburgh. The conviviality of this period is also striking. What made this possible is that it was really a tiny elite.

CC: But they must have had a way of connecting with ordinary people and therefore influencing them?

TD: Not necessarily. In Scotland the changes in the eighteenth century, in comparison with England anyway, were largely top-down. It is as if the elites in Scotland decided to grab society by the scruff of the neck and push it in a new direction.

CC: Were these elites just the landed classes?

TD: They were the power or the landed class and their relatives and associates in the legal class. We can also add in the university men, and some church men, because they were part of Scotland's educated elite. And so 'the connectors', from that elite down, especially in terms of pragmatic and practical changes, in agriculture for example, were the factors. These were men who had also been schooled in the university environment and they were often trained lawyers. In terms of my own research it is clear that this great crusade, especially for agrarian modernisation, came from above. And the irony about this is that one man's agricultural improvement was another man's clearances. What's striking about these elites is their confidence in their ability to deliver. Indeed because these people were so confident that they were right, in both the Highlands and the Lowlands, they were willing to strain the sinews of social stability. They also thought there would not be a reaction from the populace.

CC: So you are saying that the 'age of improvement' is a good example of a period of Scottish history when change was rapid and transformatory rather than slow and incremental. Could the same also be said of the Reformation or religious reforms in Scotland?

TD: No. Of course, the Reformation ultimately changed Scotland dramatically but many of the changes took years to come about. It was in many ways a gradual change. A much better example of rapid transformatory change can be seen in our own time – from the late 1970s onwards into the 1980s and 1990s. Indeed I would say that in 50 years or so future historians, looking back, will see that Scotland took a decisive change of direction during this period and that the transformation was much more rapid than it was during the age of improvement. One way to think about this change is this: in terms of social structure and value system, 1950s Scotland had much more in common with the 1850s than with our own time.

CC: How would you characterise these changes?

TD: The change I am talking about is made up of economic, social, cultural and political manifestations. The economic one is perhaps the most obvious – it is literally the revolutionary development of an economic system which is quite different from the one that had sustained Scotland since the industrial revolution. The dynamo of the old economy was heavy industry – from shipbuilding through to engineering. That economy had literally melted away by the late 1970s and 1980s. Perhaps the classic manifestation of the rapid decline of the old economy is the virtual disappearance of coal-mining. And we have to remember that these old industries were not just a source of wealth but also identity. In place of these old industries we now have finance, tourism, service industries, the provision of health and education services and the oil industry. When we put this together with the huge increase in affluence in this period, the emancipation of women and changes in family structure, then it is reasonable to talk about a revolution in Scottish society.

CC: But are you not just describing a process all industrial countries have gone through?

TD: Of course it is true that a world economic revolution has moved developed economies away from manufacturing to service industries. But it happened particularly swiftly in Scotland for two reasons. The first concerns the activities of the Thatcher government. You have to remember that the state had been bailing out Scottish industry from the period of nationalisation in 1945 on and the Tory government pulled back on that commitment. Then when the same government allowed interest rates to go through the roof in the early 1980s they effectively pulled the plug on the old economy. In other words, the result was melt-down. The second reason is the oil crisis of the early 1980s which had a similar effect.

CC: In Scotland Thatcherism is generally seen as an unmitigated disaster for the country but according to your thesis it has brought real benefit.

TD: We have an economy which is much more diversified and in tune with modern developed economies. What's more we now have an economy which plays to Scotland's strengths as it circles round our intellect, our abilities and the clear international fame of our institutions of higher education. But if we accept that we now have a better and more modern economy – one that can hold its own in the world – then it is time to revisit our understanding of Thatcherism. You are right in saying there's a tendency in Scotland to see it as something that was unambiguously evil when clearly this is not the case. There is a caveat, however. We have now moved into 'the accreditation society' with over 50 per cent going into higher education and there's a great deal of social mobility. But this is terrible for those who are not able to penetrate this new economy because they do not have the qualifications. They are almost destined to be excluded and deprived – after all so many of the old manual or semi-skilled jobs have gone. And there are other negative side-effects to the type of changes I am describing. The decline of neighbourhood and community, for example. The rise in individualism and the new impersonality of labour markets.

CC: There is little doubt that Thatcherism heightened inequality throughout the UK and Scottish poverty statistics make depressing reading, but can I just press you further on the nature of the revolution you think we are living through. Do you see it mainly confined to the economy and family structure?

TD: No, because there has also been a transformation of cultural and political attitudes. Indeed I think the recent alienation, or indifference to politics, is an inevitable reaction to all this change. The respectable upper working and middle class do not have any big issues to be overly concerned about and I think this is one of the fundamental reasons why fewer people are voting. But alongside this, paradoxically, there has been a huge reassertion of Scottish identity and again this is totally new.

CC: Thinking about the argument I put in *The Scots' Crisis of Confidence*, namely that confidence and a whole range of related attitudes such as optimism are big issues facing contemporary Scotland, is there an argument that we are living in a new world, with a different economy and devolved politics, and yet our attitudes have not changed dramatically?

TD: I certainly agree that they have not changed in proportion to it. Indeed I think we could go even further than that. I do not even think there is a consciousness among the Scottish population of the huge change which we have actually come through. This was evident to me recently at the Edinburgh Book Festival. I was involved in a Radio Scotland discussion, on a panel with the novelist Ian Rankin among others, and it was clear from both the panel members and the audience that people seem to think we are somehow stuck in the past. Which therefore begs the question, how have we managed to have a subtle or what I would call a 'velvet revolution'? The second question is this: has the attitudinal change matched the material change? And I think the classic demonstration that it has not is all the frenzied stupidity about the Scottish Parliament and the denunciation of devolution. So we still have some way to go.

CC: But the rosy picture you paint of the Scottish economy is at odds with how the media, many politicians and much of the public conversation, portray it.

TD: I agree and I do think this negative view of the Scottish economy is not in line with reality. The Scottish economy has come through a really difficult time but it is now performing well. So you are right to point out that there's a degree of pessimism in Scotland which is not really warranted.

CC: Thinking of the modern era and what you term the 'velvet revolution', who are the Scots, and I am looking for specific names, who have driven, or even argued for, these changes?

TD: There aren't any.

CC: But is not this staggering?

TD: No because this revolution which has occurred has not been induced by Scots, it has been induced by global-wide forces and accelerated by developments in Westminster under the Thatcher government. This is quite different from the Irish revolution which dates from about 1980. It has been hailed as an 'economic miracle' and it was put in place by civil society, trade unions and government. The Scottish revolution has been created by forces outside our control.

CC: So you say we have lived through a huge transformatory change in Scotland, which has brought some benefits, yet there is no single Scot who can really be credited with leading this transformation.

TD: There is a void of intellectual, political and indeed you could even say cultural leadership (even though lots of good things are happening in Scottish culture). It may well be that that epithet is still correct – No Gods and Precious Few Heroes. There was a time when, like many historians, I was fairly dismissive of the idea that individuals played an important part in history preferring instead to place much more emphasis on social forces and trends. But I have changed my views on this. I do now think that individuals play an important part. Just think about the roles of Nelson Mandela and Bishop Tutu in South Africa. History would be different without the actions of these two figures. And, of course, with the mass media, individuals if anything can exert even more power and influence than ever before. The paradox here is that we have just gone through a huge transformation in Scotland and yet cannot attach the name of one Scot and say it was driven, or even substantially influenced, by his or her vision.

CC: So perhaps it might be helpful to contrast the transformatory changes of the Enlightenment era with the modern period you have described. In the age of improvement there was an elite who brought about a radical shift not just in living conditions, work and so forth but also in attitudes – the elevation of reason which you described earlier, for example.

TD: That's right.

CC: But the current transformation is not only devoid of indigenous Scottish leadership but also confined mainly to the economy – to a rise in incomes, a change in the types of jobs people are doing and an increase in poverty and inequality. In other words it is largely about material change rather than psychological change. Is it not the case, then, that somehow we have not embraced this new world psychologically and we are still stuck in past, outdated attitudes which are somehow inappropriate for the world we inhabit?

TD: But what you are ignoring is the tremendous vibrancy of culture in Scotland. Although I do think that the media have got it wrong. They seem to see a correlation between what we could call cultural virtuosity and large sales of books etc. But some of the best work which will be permanent and long-lasting is being done by people who could be described as 'arcane'. Again if you try to quantify a whole range of cultural activities – film, music, painting, literature – there is no comparison between the Scotland of today and 40 years ago. In other words, whaur's your confidence problem the noo?

CC: I agree that the arts and culture scene in Scotland has been revitalised in recent years but there are whole swathes of Scottish life which have not. As you know, I have worked in organisations for many years doing training and development work and there's little doubt that organisations suffer in Scotland because people are not prepared to speak out, or even participate in decision-making. Indeed I would go so far as to say that in whole areas of Scottish life there is a 'heads-down' culture. It is even acute in some universities. I was talking to an employer in Scotland only last week and he was complaining that his workforce here, in contrast with Manchester, is very passive. I regularly talk to people from abroad who are living and working in Scotland and one of the things which strikes them forcibly about Scottish organisations is how hierarchical they are. We might pride ourselves on egalitarianism and the democratic intellect but we do not tend to run our organisations in harmony with these values. Earlier you talked about the changes in the eighteenth and nineteenth centuries and said that, in comparison with England they were very top-down. As a historian and a modern-day Scot would you say that for all the talk about equality and democracy in Scotland our society and institutions have been, and still are, hierarchical?

TD: It is not hierarchical in the eighteenth-century sense. Birth inheritance is no longer a factor and it has been replaced by a meritocratic system. But I think it is true that there is still a greater respect for authority in Scotland than in other parts of the world.

CC: One of the things about hierarchy is that it is not good at instilling a sense of personal responsibility or confidence in people. And this might be one of the reasons why there is an issue about confidence in Scotland.

TD: I agree that individual Scots may have an issue with confidence but it certainly cannot be a crisis. The evidence of modern Scotland is against you here – just look at how dynamic it has become.

CC: But people living in Scotland do not experience that dynamism – they do experience the confidence issue. Talk to any foreigner in Scotland and while they will like lots of things about our culture most think it is bizarre that we apologise all the time, are embarrassed at personal success and do not like drawing attention to ourselves. Most Americans pick up within a week that it is unacceptable to say anything positive about yourself and are fairly horrified at how cruel our humour can be. At the Book Festival event you mentioned earlier was it not the case that most of the audience believed that confidence *is* an issue facing Scotland?

TD: The majority did. But that is, as I said earlier, because people wrongly believe we are somehow stuck in the past.

CC: What I am really struck by when I give talks is the great thirst for a real and meaningful change in attitudes. And this has surprised me. When I was in the process of writing my book, I felt very fearful of what the reaction might be. After all, I was taking some of the great sacred cows of Scottish culture – our collectivist values, our emphasis on equality and the importance we attach to Scottish identity – and I am questioning them. I am also giving weight to the importance of psychology and attitude change in a country where most people who have consciously tried to transform Scotland have viewed political change as the sole solution.

TD: So you are saying that most people who are disgruntled with Scotland tend to see constitutional change as the answer?

CC: Yes. So you can understand why prior to publication I really thought that I would be attacked vociferously for what I had written. I particularly thought I would be done in by 'the wee hard men' that Alasdair Gray so beautifully describes. But it has not happened. What I find instead when I give a talk is that people listen intently and then agree wholeheartedly that some of our beliefs are self-defeating. Most of the Scots I have spoken to completely agree with my contention that there are two competing pressures within the culture. The first is to prove your worth. (In Scotland there is no automatic assumption of the worthiness of individuals. You have to prove it through your deeds and actions.) If you do not then you risk being seen as worthless. No doubt this is why the Scots can be very competitive. But the second pressure acts as a check on this. And that is the pressure not to stand out or get above yourself. If you obey the first pressure to achieve, there is someone holding on to your jacket at the back whispering in your ear 'don't think you're anybody special' and warning you of the all the problems which might ensue if you put your head above the parapet and then 'get it wrong'. When Scots leave

Scotland and are freed up of the 'jacket pullers' they achieve much more than they do if they stay at home. In fact, most Scots who have lived abroad for a while are horrified by the conformity of modern day Scotland. Part of my mission for Scotland is to contribute to the creation of a cultural environment in which people feel they can be themselves. I would like to see an environment where people feel it is easier to express their views and not feel afraid they are going to get 'it' wrong. I would also like to see a much bigger political spectrum, with lots of different opinions and viewpoints being expressed.

TD: Of course, I accept that the transformation Scotland has gone through has not been root and branch – that it has transformed some areas more than others. But I still think you are overstating your case and underestimating the change which has actually taken place.

CC: But does it not depend on what we are looking at? If you are looking at the economy and incomes – yes. But the change is less profound if you are looking at attitudes to self and others – and confidence issues.

TD: So are you trying to say we are both right?

CC: Of course. I wholeheartedly agree that we have lived through a huge amount of economic and material change. I just do not think that there has been a concomitant shift in attitudes. But I think we are getting to the tipping point and that when attitudinal change happens in Scotland it will come quickly. And then you will really see a revolution in Scottish society. In fact, I might be able to say to you 'whaur's your velvet revolution, the noo?'

Carol Craig is Chief Executive of the Centre for Confidence and Well-Being and author of The Scots' Crisis of Confidence.
Tom Devine is Director of the Research Institute of Irish and Scottish Studies at the University of Aberdeen, and author of The Scottish Nation 1700–2000 *and* Scotland's Empire.

23. Scotland in the Global Age

Tom Nairn in conversation with George Kerevan

Edinburgh
5 October 2004

Dear Tom,

I feel like an old soldier parading for the Armistice, medals proudly on show, but just a bit quizzical about what we achieved in the conflict. For you and I are battle-scarred veterans of the Second Devolutionary War. The one that ran from the failure of the first devolution referendum in 1979, to the final victory and restoration of the Scottish Parliament in 1999.

A period when Scottish politics, far from forsaking the constitutional question, saw it dominate. A period when civic Scotland mobilised as at no time since the great split in the Church of Scotland in 1843. We faced down Thatcher, turned the original Labourist compromise of a Scottish Assembly into a full-blown legislative parliament with tax-varying powers, dented the hallowed sovereignty of Westminster for the first time in three centuries, and annihilated the once hegemonic Tory Party north of the border.

But the guns are silent now. For the reality of devolution has seen half the electorate flee the ballot box at only the second Scottish Parliament election. Has seen the Scottish economy continue to under-perform the UK average exactly as it did before constitutional change. Has seen the cultural intelligentsia abandon politics for either well-paid light entertainment or gloomy personal introspection.

We need to situate the current uncertain phase of Scottish and British constitutional evolution deeper in the tectonic forces shaping British and global politics.

As good a place as any to begin is the old agenda you and Perry Anderson developed in the *New Left Review* of the 1960s. British society was desperate for economic and social reform – a reform delayed both by a reactionary Tory Party and an Establishment-hugging Labour Party. Your own path-breaking book, *The Break-up of Britain* (1977), was seized on by many of us as a manifesto for how to get out of this historical impasse. A Scottish breakaway – made economically viable with the discovery of North Sea oil – was not a nationalist deviation but a necessary step in the modernising revolution. Ditto regional movements in France and Spain.

How then has devolution in practice failed to open the floodgates to real social and economic change? Let me offer a few pointers to start the discussion.

First, none of us guessed that, in the face of economic stasis, the modernising revolution would begin on the right. Thatcher was a British (or English) de Gaulle, restructuring capital and smashing the worst elements of Stalinist trades unionism. A new bloc of the English professional middle classes and labour aristocracy responded to this liberation from the moribund state machine, ensuring Blair would carry on in the same fashion. The fall of the Iron Curtain and ensuing economic globalisation ended any hope of a utopian British socialist state, or even a social democratic British Federation.

At this point, history played its cruellest trick. Many of the most conservative forces in Scotland, in retreat from Thatcherism and Blairism, turned to devolution as a mechanism for defending vested interests and corporatism. So we have the highest per capita health spending in Europe and the worst health. Twenty per cent fewer young Scots finish high school than the European average. Over half of GDP is in the state sector. And the same old clique is in charge. A similar reactionary fate has befallen much else in Blair's constitutional agenda.

Tom, we won the Second Devolutionary War but, like so many before us, we lost the peace. Why?

George

Melbourne
19 October 2004

Dear George,
Although it's kind of you to refer back to Perry Anderson and *The Break-up of Britain*, these no longer measure up to what you rightly call 'the tectonic forces shaping British and global politics'. Actually, existing 'internationalism' has changed everything. I suspect the real disagreement between us lies less on 'the matter of Scotland' than on where that matter now stands in a global context.

Scotland finds itself on the growing list of countries seeking self-government under the conditions of first-stage globalisation. They extend from Wales to Corsica, then from Palestine via Kurdistan to Sri Lanka, Tibet, Taiwan, parts of Indonesia, and then across Melanesia from Hawaii to the most remote place on earth. Easter Island is now demanding 'autonomy' from Chile. Since 9/11 and the explosive affirmation of American nationalism, these issues have become the substance of the globalising process – what comes after the End of History.

You talk of a 'modernising revolution' from the right, that unfortunately coincided with Devolution. But surely there was no such *revolution*. There were cumulative, even radical, social and economic shifts from the right, organically linked to the capitalist expansion of the later Cold War period. Under *détente*, such expansion encountered ever-fewer obstacles, as West and East put stability and continuity before everything else – both to avoid thermonuclear war, and to prevent any recurrence of the deplorable anarchy of the 1960s. Right- and left-wing historical materialisms (and ruling classes) agreed on one thing: disorder from below must be banned.

This agreement was the key to *actual* globalisation after 1989. It was a recipe not for revolution but for prolonged and successful *counter-revolution*. The Reaganites saw the Stalinists off, and inherited the earth. Neither provided a commendable diet for humane globalisation. Revolutions are essentially political; counter-revolutions are in essence anti-political, relying on the containment and castration of democratic agency, and its replacement with apathy, mass cynicism and privatisation.

So where does devolved Scotland stand, vis-à-vis the long counter-revolution? Your stance seems to me extraordinarily glum. 'The same old clique in charge?' The 'reactionary fate' of Blair's (and McConnell's) reforming agenda? But of course that was the intention of devolution, and of the 'Scotostan' it set up – to 'strengthen Britain', as John Reid never tires of reminding us. It is to the credit of the Scottish electorate that it has shown definite signs of rejection and defiance. The 2003 Holyrood election was a defeat for both Old and New Labour and old-style Nationalism. Green politics, post-Leninist socialism, and independents have all emerged, and in association with important living sectors of the Labour and Liberal Democratic movements, could now form a quite different sort of national movement.

So let's get on with it. But *we can*! In fact, we can do it by 2007. The nature of actually existing internationalism demands more civic–democratic nationality politics, not less. In the Scottish case, it needs a broader alliance – analogous to the old Constitutional Convention you refer to, but bolder in its aims and ideas, and more in tune with the times. The great breaking tide of a more united globe is now on our side, rather than against it. It was only the miserable British–American counterfeit of 'globalisation' that pretended otherwise.

Tom

Edinburgh
22 October 2004

Dear Tom,
I see I am branded a pessimist over devolution! You, however, seem to be stretching optimism of the will in an absurdly idealist direction.

Can we perhaps agree on the following: that the complex process we call 'globalisation' has, since 1989, changed the terms of the debate on UK devolution and the wider 'national question'.

This globalisation is rooted in deep economic and cultural changes: the dramatic extension of the world market to incorporate China and the ex-Soviet Union; a massive speeding up of the technological cycle; the creation of a global 24-hour news culture dominated by the English language; a quantum leap in the mobility of both capital and labour on a world scale, afforded by the new communications technology; and mass proletarianisation and urbanisation on a scale only fantasised about in the Communist Manifesto, but also the creation of a mass intelligentsia and white collar middle class.

This is the underlying material basis for a 'second wave' of nationalism (distinct from the simple 'modernisation' agenda of proto-national elites, as originally espoused by Ernest Gellner and yourself). The first wave of nationalism in the nineteenth and twentieth centuries was essentially a catching-up process with Western Europe and North America. The second wave – which overlaps the first – is driven by the need to detach regional economies (some very advanced) from their existing nation state 'shell' and re-orient them directly to the new global markets and circuits of capital.

This process affects everyone, including the United States. For instance, LA and New York have virtually detached themselves from the US hinterland and become *de facto* hubs of an integrated global economy. LA is the capital of South East Asia and of cyberspace, while industrial regions in the US like Ohio have shrunk to internal economic colonies of the global hubs.

At the UK level, London has already broken away and become

virtually a separate economy driven by the needs of globalisation. As a result it has also become the most cosmopolitan culture in the shell of the old Britain, a global hub dealing with other global hubs.

The Scottish economy – traditionally one of the most open in Europe – has become more globalised than ever. Besides oil, whisky and high tech, the rise of giant banks like the RBS group (with its growing stake in the US) and international energy utilities like Scottish Power has oriented business relentlessly away from England and directly towards the outside world. In this scenario, London taxes and London interest rates are an unwelcome encumbrance.

But in defiance of globalising pressures, the new Scottish Executive has ignored the Scottish economy – unlike practically every other regional government in the EU. Instead, it has pursued an old-fashioned redistributive agenda, driving the share of the state in GDP to over 50 per cent, and drawing available scarce labour into a burgeoning state machine reminiscent of the UK in the 1970s. As a result, Scottish economic growth crawls along at an average of 1.5 per cent per annum. The political conundrum is not when the motley collection of Trots, Greens, rural Lib Dems and independents seize power in the Scottish Parliament, but why a youthful, nationalist, free market party of the type seen in the Baltic States has not yet appeared in Scotland.

Constitutional reform, however, which in Britain has concentrated on the ad hoc dismantling of traditional institutions, has helped to release centrifugal forces by removing the glue of national unity, just when such globalist forces are transforming the nation from below. Enter a phalanx of populist parties such as Ukip and the BNP. Tom: yes, the electorate are fed up with mainstream democratic politics but history is rather cruel to those who assume that it always takes a progressive form, even in Scotland.

North of the border, the SNP has been in apparent retreat since Devolution but the underlying national question has not gone away. Part of the reason lies in the balance of forces within the devolution settlement. Labour first seized on asymmetric devolution (as opposed to federalism) as an ad hoc policy to head off the rise of the Scottish

National Party in the 1970s. But during the Thatcher years Labour greatly extended the scope of devolution from a minimalist regional assembly to a legislative parliament with tax-varying powers, as a crude bulwark against any recurring Tory majority at Westminster.

During this period, many Scottish interests switched from being anti-devolution to supporting it, expressly on the grounds it would protect them from pro-market or anti-monopoly reforms being pursued by Thatcher and her heirs (among whom I include Tony Blair). For instance, the Scottish universities, which originally had opposed administrative devolution, in case it reduced their status vis-à-vis English higher education, shifted ground when they thought a Scottish Parliament would better protect their financial interests and academic independence.

Devolution north of the border (and in Wales) has turned out to be a re-institutionalisation of vested interests, and it is in that sense that it has proved reactionary and a roadblock to modernisation.

The previous Union Settlement of 1707 also preserved Scottish vested interests within the United Kingdom context. Various Scottish elites kept their Kirk, education system and law courts in return for not challenging London politically. But today London has already ceded economically from the old-style UK, while Scotland's vested interests cannot go on indefinitely milking subsidies from the old system. In that context, devolution is fascinating because it has introduced a national political forum into Scotland that must eventually provide a platform for nascent modernising forces.

Devolution is a pressure cooker with globalisation providing the fire underneath. That's why, in the end, I am an optimist of the will.

George

Melbourne
30 October 2004

Dear George,
Neoliberalism's recent dominance has frozen the capacity to conceive of radical political action by adopting the mantle of radicalism for itself.

The outstanding voice of nineteenth-century political reflection, Alexis de Tocqueville, put it best:

> *After believing that we could transform ourselves (during the Enlightenment), we now believe that even the slightest reform is impossible. After excessive pride, we have fallen into an equally excessive humility. Once we thought ourselves capable of everything; today we believe ourselves capable of nothing. It pleases us to believe that from now on struggle and effort are futile, that our blood, our bodies, and our nervous systems will always prevail over our will and capacity. This is the peculiar argument of our time. . . .It will drive your contemporaries, who are already weak, to an even greater weakness.*
>
> Cited here from R Wolin, *The Seduction of Unreason*
> (Princeton: Princeton University Press, 2004), p 293

The peculiar argument of that time has become a general disposition of our own. And it has a special relevance in Scotland – a country historically disposed towards exactly the weakness Tocqueville diagnosed. The trouble with the Scots isn't their economic failure, on which you're right, but also give far too much importance to. It is a profounder political nervelessness deriving from the surrender and self-colonisation of the eighteenth and later centuries – 'lack of self-confidence', the true justified sinner of post-1707 Scotland.

The neoliberal ruling classes of post-1989 had the good luck to inherit such a deep-died apoliticism. All they had to do was water it with daily newspaper and TV fertiliser, and the odd electoral bribe nobody could refuse. With strong support from the American Enterprise Institute, neoliberalism's version of determinism now claims patent rights for 'globalisation'. This is hustlerdom at its most brazen. The matrix of globalisation has hardly begun to develop.

You conclude by saying the new Holyrood Parliament is a 'pressure cooker with globalisation providing the fire underneath'. Hence the latter is bound to determine Scotland's exit towards exemplary neoliberal statehood – once 'nascent modernising forces' have dealt with your impressive list of inherited institutional deadbeats.

But the imagery remains revealingly misleading. At the end of 2004, we are not sitting quietly observing pressure-cookers coming to the boil on assorted stove-tops. We're in the middle of a bloody chip-pan fire. The hottest single part is in Iraq where, as I write, part of what's left of the Scottish army is being hurried up to Baghdad to help President Bush's failure appear less shameful and carnage-strewn.

But more generally it can also be said (in Amy Chua's words) that *the world is on fire*. The deformed mode of globalisation that took hold in the 1990s is responsible, and there are discomfiting echoes of it in your stance. You say the main question is not 'when the motley collection of Trots, Greens, rural Lib Dems and independents seize power', but why we don't possess a responsible, free-market-trained nationalist movement like some in Eastern Europe. This is over-familiar rhetoric, carrying us back to the days when Thatcher and Reagan were just warming up. Shouldn't it be buried along with them?

The main *question* is when Scots (whose situation is unlike the East, just as it has always been unlike ex-colonised peoples) will get the chance to do the one thing that matters. Which is, to *vote for themselves*. Or, put in another way, to vote themselves back into political existence. This unavoidably motley, or broad-based, constitutional matter is unlikely to be channelled via a single party or leader. It needs the Parliament to do it, supported by as many stane-pebblers as can be assembled for action outside it. Alas, I'm too far away for stanes to have much impact, but you have the luck to be just across the road.

Tom

Edinburgh
31 October 2004

Dear Tom,

As I remove your metaphorical barbs from my bleeding flesh, let us agree to differ on our judgements regarding the globalisation process of the last decades. You see the 'anti-globalists' as reinserting politics (human agency) back into history; I see them as profoundly reactionary. However, where we have common cause is in this: globalisation, far from sweeping away nation states, is reinforcing the need for people, at quite an organic level, to create new democratic structures in response to the dramatic interconnections of global society. In Scotland I see the conditions for a democratic resurgence growing in several ways.

Part of this involves strengthened regional blocks – an enlarged EU, a reinvigorated if rickety African Union, and the newly dynamic Association of South East Asian Nations (ASEAN, which is starting to think about a common currency). Even more so, it involves a resurgence of small-nation nationalism, bolstered with instant internet and digital television intercourse with the rest of humanity.

This small-nation nationalism can be found elsewhere; the best examples may lie in Quebec and in Catalonia. But what is striking about both places is that the traditional nationalist forces, recently in apparent decline, are finding new political energy in the inability of their surrounding nation states to respond adequately to the challenges presented by globalisation.

Far from 'normalising' politics within the Union, five years of devolution have continued to divide Scotland from the rest of the UK. First, the Scottish Parliament continues to garner new powers ad hoc as a result of constitutional impasse at Westminster, eg the recent transfer of strategic rail functions. Despite the local cynicism over the cost of the new Scottish Parliament building, and despite the high abstentions at the second Parliamentary elections in 2003, every opinion poll confirms the Scottish electorate wants more powers repatriated to Holyrood from Westminster. And the major repercussion of the debacle over the new Parliament building – which came in at ten times its original cost – is the call for a new, more efficient Scottish civil service entirely separate from Whitehall.

Second, the Scottish Parliament has introduced a significant political reform by legislating for proportional representation in local government, using the single transferable vote (STV) method, to be implemented in 2007. This reform will have dramatic political repercussions: it will end the hegemony of the Labour Party at local level and force coalition politics on every major town hall; it will also give the SNP as many as several hundred additional local councillors. So far, Labour has systematically avoided any pacts at local level with the SNP, but PR in the town halls means that some day the nationalists are bound to become a serious force in Scotland's industrial central belt.

Third, the Scottish media continues to adapt to the requirements of a specifically Scottish political debate. For instance, while the merger of Carlton and Granada has created a single UK ITV – swallowing up Welsh ITV in the process – Scottish Television remains under separate ownership. The Scottish press has also altered: devolution forced a number of London papers to create quite distinct (and bolshie) Scottish editions edited north of the border. In the forefront are the *Daily Telegraph* and (of all papers) the *Daily Mail*. Curiously, the left-wing *Guardian* and *Independent* have virtually ignored Scotland, possibly because the indigenous media is relatively left of centre.

However, these Scottish developments are demarcated from the experience in Quebec and Catalonia. They reflect a largely internal political dynamic that deliberately does not challenge the rest of the UK, whereas the other 'stateless' nationalisms have become adept at using their parliamentary institutions, restricted as they may be, to pursue external and international goals. This is the boundary that must be crossed in order to create a genuine Scottish national self-awareness and self-interest. Or in your terms, Tom, for Scotland to challenge its alleged lack of self-confidence, or 'vote itself back into existence'.

The obvious absence in post-devolutionary politics in the UK, as compared with the Continent, has been the reluctance of the devolved assemblies to operate in alliance to extract concessions from central government. London, Scotland, Wales and Northern Ireland have a combined population that is roughly one in three of the UK population – a weighty political block. Even missing out the on–off Northern Ireland Assembly, the other three administrations are all led by Labour politicians who could easily collaborate more.

The same absence of a systematic regional foreign policy is found in relation to the European Union. Why this absence of an external policy dimension, especially given my thesis that regions like Scotland are being forced by economic developments to ally directly with the world marketplace rather than mediate through their existing nation states? There are some obvious political barriers. The most distinctive of these is the Barnett mechanism for allocating public expenditure to Scotland, Wales and Northern Ireland.

Under the Barnett Formula, any percentage increase in Treasury spending for England is automatically allocated to the Celtic regions pro rata by a fixed formula roughly linked to population. The three regions each started with higher per capita public spending than England; in Scotland it is around 20 per cent. Over time, Barnett should reduce this differential. But Scotland's rapidly falling population (in the absence of any change to the Barnett index) means per capita public spending in Scotland remains wildly in excess of England – even making allowance for factors such as poorer health and vastly lower population density. Few Scottish politicians want to interfere with a political goose that lays such golden eggs. An independent Scottish 'foreign policy' – say, ganging up with other UK industrial regions to get lower corporation tax than England, as occasionally floated in Northern Ireland – would risk an English backlash that threatened to dismantle Barnett.

But there is an alternative to Barnett and it lurks near the surface of every constitutional debate in Scotland – the idea of fiscal autonomy for the Scottish Parliament. That is, Scotland collecting all or the majority of its funding from local taxes, while paying into the Exchequer for national activities such as defence. The current fiscal model in Britain, where the UK regions receive fully three-quarters of their financial needs from central government, ensures the regions must ultimately toe the line. But even in centralist France, where Paris still likes to run the show, the regions raise 47 per cent of their income from their own taxes, plus another 19 per cent from various charges they levy, leaving only a third of the cash coming from central government.

Ignored down south, fiscal autonomy is the hot topic in Scottish politics. It is viewed sympathetically by Labour modernisers such as Wendy Alexander MSP, who see it as a way of breaking the hold of old-style Labour clientelism and corporatism. By the SNP who see it as a Trojan horse for independence. And even by free-market Tory MSPs, who see it as a way of imposing fiscal discipline on the profligate Scottish Executive. Fiscal autonomy will be the battleground for the next stage in Scottish devolution.

As I write this, I can see the exotic new Scottish Parliament building outside my office window. Unfortunately, during the many expensive redesigns, the civil servants added a massive concrete wall to foil would-be terrorists. The wall lies between me and our nascent Scottish democracy. There's another metaphor in there somewhere.

George

Melbourne
4 November 2004

Dear George,
There's no longer all the time in the world for Scots, or anyone else. Thanks to globalisation, the wingèd chariot is forcing all nations into altered consciousness and action – not merely the Americans, Brits and Australians, and the victims of their concerted good will in Iraq and Kurdistan.

I agree, 'dramatic interconnections and changes in global society' do render 'new democratic structures' a priority. These may now be more than narrowly national; but they also remain national – and sometimes nationalist – in their source, their initiative and their potential popularity.

It's interesting how different our respective emphases remain. Yours invariably focuses on the international and economic – in effect, upon the forced transcendence that post-1989 globalisation has imposed, and made irreversible. My own leans towards the constitutional – whatever re-knitted relationships between peoples and their states could move things forward, and away from the crippling anachronisms represented by today's American, British and Australian politics.

Globalisation is double-edged; its in-built contradictions cannot freely work themselves through, because it remains caged within a sclerotic, backward-fixated *political* world. In some ways, it has been forced back into the cage, above all since 9/11.

You argue that nations like Scotland, Quebec and Catalonia need to participate more directly in the wider post-Cold War world, and deploy their own foreign and trade policies. While agreeing, I would qualify this by pointing out that, in these and other cases, such external initiatives depend on some political reinforcement of respective national identities. It is constitutional shifts that got them this far: more are needed to take them further.

This factor is oddly absent from your practical ruminations. Yet, in Scottish terms, is there any doubt at all that, over the last 30 years or so, by far the most aggressive and unrelenting form of nationalism has been the *British* one? Robertson, Reid, Dewar and their followers were not content to beat nationalists politically: over and over again, they said they wanted to *kill them stone dead*. Mercifully, such a fate was not literally practicable in the UK (as it has been, for instance, in Indonesia's East Timor). What the Brit-nats wanted was to kill a political (and constitutional) idea. Far from being a quirk, such sadism is the normal expression of established authority, *above all when supported by national minorities* that have switched allegiance to the majority or host culture. Both psychologically and socially, any minority national who casts his or her lot in this way is compelled to overdo it.

In this situation of staved-off break-up, the most practical issue before us is the development of a new Scottish identity of departure. The SNP has been unavoidably deeply configured by that same dilemma. All-British identity is so strongly implanted among Scots that political nationalism has over nearly three generations learned to defend itself by a compensatory tactic, now itself traditional – in effect, by a style of sectarianism and rigid *partinost*, or party-firstism. Salmond's restored edition of Nationalism is curiously like Brown's Labourism: myth-history tarted up as Salvation to come. I mean, how *British* can you get?

You point out how the electorates of Quebec and Catalonia have moved ahead of their parties. But so have the Scots. In 2003 they definitely misbehaved, showing marked impatience with a set menu of Granny's half-reheated stovies. New parties and movements turned serious. New voices proclaimed belief in *their own* versions of independence, socialism and Greenery. This wind of change is by far the most *practical* factor on the scene. As you say, it has since then won another victory, the reform of local government voting.

The most important feature of this turning will be to make a Scottish political system integrally more democratic than the UK one. This, plus the fiscal autonomy you argue so strongly for, would make a strong basis for the independence bid. Both democracy and tax-powers are death to the Barnett Formula's weird echo of feudalism.

What I meant by 'voting for ourselves' in such a context is supporting a *constitutional right*, in advance of any attempts to dismount from the UK's constitutional carriage. This may appear an odd notion – usually, most new states have claimed independence first, then proceeded to bestow (or inflict) a constitution upon their new citizens. Yet I don't think it's any odder than the history of the Scots – who are of course not a new state, but one of the oldest. Scottish 'nationalism' is only claiming the repatriation (as it were) of its own Elgin marbles. This historical right, if reaffirmed demo-cratically, would in turn give any Scottish government the right to hold a referendum on, eg replacement of the Treaty of Union, on a British confederation (or 'association' as the SNP has always called it) or separate Scottish membership of the European Union. Incidentally, I don't see how Westminster could *prevent* any Holyrood Parliament from consulting its own electorate on this matter, however many fits were thrown.

Fiscal autonomy plus an integrally different political system would mean *de facto* independence; and the constitutional imprimatur would make movement to a *de jure* recognition possible.

In a public speech before the last election, Sean Connery made a plea for equality of treatment and regard: Scotland should become like other nations. The only drawback to this claim was that it left open what 'nation' means. What we want is William McIlvanney's twenty-first century mongrel, mixed-up and proud of it, 'open' to the expanding world of really existing internationalism, and able to distinguish this from being Blair's (or Bush's) gun-dog.

Devolution has been a real advance, but remains fatally mired in the past of 'The Thin Red Line', the enforcement of 'Great Britain's do's and don'ts'. That past caught up with us again in 2003; let it be for the very last time. Globalisation both needs and calls for something more, and better; independence and European confederation are signposts towards it.

Tom

George Kerevan is Associate Editor of the Scotsman. *Tom Nairn is Research Professor in Globalisation at Royal Melbourne Institute of Technology and author of* The Break-up of Britain, After Britain *and* Pariah: misfortunes of the British Kingdom.

DEMOS – Licence to Publish

THE WORK (AS DEFINED BELOW) IS PROVIDED UNDER THE TERMS OF THIS LICENCE ("LICENCE"). THE WORK IS PROTECTED BY COPYRIGHT AND/OR OTHER APPLICABLE LAW. ANY USE OF THE WORK OTHER THAN AS AUTHORIZED UNDER THIS LICENCE IS PROHIBITED. BY EXERCISING ANY RIGHTS TO THE WORK PROVIDED HERE, YOU ACCEPT AND AGREE TO BE BOUND BY THE TERMS OF THIS LICENCE. DEMOS GRANTS YOU THE RIGHTS CONTAINED HERE IN CONSIDERATION OF YOUR ACCEPTANCE OF SUCH TERMS AND CONDITIONS.

1. **Definitions**
   a **"Collective Work"** means a work, such as a periodical issue, anthology or encyclopedia, in which the Work in its entirety in unmodified form, along with a number of other contributions, constituting separate and independent works in themselves, are assembled into a collective whole. A work that constitutes a Collective Work will not be considered a Derivative Work (as defined below) for the purposes of this Licence.
   b **"Derivative Work"** means a work based upon the Work or upon the Work and other pre-existing works, such as a musical arrangement, dramatization, fictionalization, motion picture version, sound recording, art reproduction, abridgment, condensation, or any other form in which the Work may be recast, transformed, or adapted, except that a work that constitutes a Collective Work or a translation from English into another language will not be considered a Derivative Work for the purpose of this Licence.
   c **"Licensor"** means the individual or entity that offers the Work under the terms of this Licence.
   d **"Original Author"** means the individual or entity who created the Work.
   e **"Work"** means the copyrightable work of authorship offered under the terms of this Licence.
   f **"You"** means an individual or entity exercising rights under this Licence who has not previously violated the terms of this Licence with respect to the Work, or who has received express permission from DEMOS to exercise rights under this Licence despite a previous violation.
2. **Fair Use Rights.** Nothing in this licence is intended to reduce, limit, or restrict any rights arising from fair use, first sale or other limitations on the exclusive rights of the copyright owner under copyright law or other applicable laws.
3. **Licence Grant.** Subject to the terms and conditions of this Licence, Licensor hereby grants You a worldwide, royalty-free, non-exclusive, perpetual (for the duration of the applicable copyright) licence to exercise the rights in the Work as stated below:
   a to reproduce the Work, to incorporate the Work into one or more Collective Works, and to reproduce the Work as incorporated in the Collective Works;
   b to distribute copies or phonorecords of, display publicly, perform publicly, and perform publicly by means of a digital audio transmission the Work including as incorporated in Collective Works;
   The above rights may be exercised in all media and formats whether now known or hereafter devised. The above rights include the right to make such modifications as are technically necessary to exercise the rights in other media and formats. All rights not expressly granted by Licensor are hereby reserved.
4. **Restrictions.** The licence granted in Section 3 above is expressly made subject to and limited by the following restrictions:
   a You may distribute, publicly display, publicly perform, or publicly digitally perform the Work only under the terms of this Licence, and You must include a copy of, or the Uniform Resource Identifier for, this Licence with every copy or phonorecord of the Work You distribute, publicly display, publicly perform, or publicly digitally perform. You may not offer or impose any terms on the Work that alter or restrict the terms of this Licence or the recipients' exercise of the rights granted hereunder. You may not sublicence the Work. You must keep intact all notices that refer to this Licence and to the disclaimer of warranties. You may not distribute, publicly display, publicly perform, or publicly digitally perform the Work with any technological measures that control access or use of the Work in a manner inconsistent with the terms of this Licence Agreement. The above applies to the Work as incorporated in a Collective Work, but this does not require the Collective Work apart from the Work itself to be made subject to the terms of this Licence. If You create a Collective Work, upon notice from any Licencor You must, to the extent practicable, remove from the Collective Work any reference to such Licensor or the Original Author, as requested.
   b You may not exercise any of the rights granted to You in Section 3 above in any manner that is primarily intended for or directed toward commercial advantage or private monetary

compensation. The exchange of the Work for other copyrighted works by means of digital file-sharing or otherwise shall not be considered to be intended for or directed toward commercial advantage or private monetary compensation, provided there is no payment of any monetary compensation in connection with the exchange of copyrighted works.

c If you distribute, publicly display, publicly perform, or publicly digitally perform the Work or any Collective Works, You must keep intact all copyright notices for the Work and give the Original Author credit reasonable to the medium or means You are utilizing by conveying the name (or pseudonym if applicable) of the Original Author if supplied; the title of the Work if supplied. Such credit may be implemented in any reasonable manner; provided, however, that in the case of a Collective Work, at a minimum such credit will appear where any other comparable authorship credit appears and in a manner at least as prominent as such other comparable authorship credit.

5. Representations, Warranties and Disclaimer

a By offering the Work for public release under this Licence, Licensor represents and warrants that, to the best of Licensor's knowledge after reasonable inquiry:

   i Licensor has secured all rights in the Work necessary to grant the licence rights hereunder and to permit the lawful exercise of the rights granted hereunder without You having any obligation to pay any royalties, compulsory licence fees, residuals or any other payments;

   ii The Work does not infringe the copyright, trademark, publicity rights, common law rights or any other right of any third party or constitute defamation, invasion of privacy or other tortious injury to any third party.

b EXCEPT AS EXPRESSLY STATED IN THIS LICENCE OR OTHERWISE AGREED IN WRITING OR REQUIRED BY APPLICABLE LAW, THE WORK IS LICENCED ON AN "AS IS" BASIS, WITHOUT WARRANTIES OF ANY KIND, EITHER EXPRESS OR IMPLIED INCLUDING, WITHOUT LIMITATION, ANY WARRANTIES REGARDING THE CONTENTS OR ACCURACY OF THE WORK.

6. Limitation on Liability. EXCEPT TO THE EXTENT REQUIRED BY APPLICABLE LAW, AND EXCEPT FOR DAMAGES ARISING FROM LIABILITY TO A THIRD PARTY RESULTING FROM BREACH OF THE WARRANTIES IN SECTION 5, IN NO EVENT WILL LICENSOR BE LIABLE TO YOU ON ANY LEGAL THEORY FOR ANY SPECIAL, INCIDENTAL, CONSEQUENTIAL, PUNITIVE OR EXEMPLARY DAMAGES ARISING OUT OF THIS LICENCE OR THE USE OF THE WORK, EVEN IF LICENSOR HAS BEEN ADVISED OF THE POSSIBILITY OF SUCH DAMAGES.

7. Termination

a This Licence and the rights granted hereunder will terminate automatically upon any breach by You of the terms of this Licence. Individuals or entities who have received Collective Works from You under this Licence, however, will not have their licences terminated provided such individuals or entities remain in full compliance with those licences. Sections 1, 2, 5, 6, 7, and 8 will survive any termination of this Licence.

b Subject to the above terms and conditions, the licence granted here is perpetual (for the duration of the applicable copyright in the Work). Notwithstanding the above, Licensor reserves the right to release the Work under different licence terms or to stop distributing the Work at any time; provided, however that any such election will not serve to withdraw this Licence (or any other licence that has been, or is required to be, granted under the terms of this Licence), and this Licence will continue in full force and effect unless terminated as stated above.

8. Miscellaneous

a Each time You distribute or publicly digitally perform the Work or a Collective Work, DEMOS offers to the recipient a licence to the Work on the same terms and conditions as the licence granted to You under this Licence.

b If any provision of this Licence is invalid or unenforceable under applicable law, it shall not affect the validity or enforceability of the remainder of the terms of this Licence, and without further action by the parties to this agreement, such provision shall be reformed to the minimum extent necessary to make such provision valid and enforceable.

c No term or provision of this Licence shall be deemed waived and no breach consented to unless such waiver or consent shall be in writing and signed by the party to be charged with such waiver or consent.

d This Licence constitutes the entire agreement between the parties with respect to the Work licensed here. There are no understandings, agreements or representations with respect to the Work not specified here. Licensor shall not be bound by any additional provisions that may appear in any communication from You. This Licence may not be modified without the mutual written agreement of DEMOS and You.